MARC-ANTOINE CHARPENTIER

Oxford Studies of Composers (23)

MARC-ANTOINE CHARPENTIER

H. WILEY HITCHCOCK

Oxford New York
OXFORD UNIVERSITY PRESS
1990

Oxford University Press, Walton Street, Oxford OX2 6DP

Oxford New York Toronto
Delhi Bombay Calcutta Madras Karachi
Petaling Jaya Singapore Hong Kong Tokyo
Nairobi Dar es Salaam Cape Town
Melbourne Auckland
and associated companies in
Berlin Ibadan

Oxford is a trade mark of Oxford University Press

Published in the United States
by Oxford University Press, New York

British Library Cataloguing in Publication Data
Hitchcock, H. Wiley (Hugh Wiley), 1923–
Marc-Antoine Charpentier. (Oxford studies of
composers; 23)
1. French music. Charpentier, Marc-Antoine, 1704.
Critical studies
I. Title   II. Series
780'.92'4
ISBN 0–19–316410–8 (Pbk.)
ISBN 0–19–316411–6

Library of Congress Cataloging-in-Publication Data
Hitchcock, H. Wiley (Hugh Wiley), 1923–
Marc-Antoine Charpentier/H. Wiley Hitchcock.
(Oxford studies of composers; 23)
Includes bibliographical references.
1. Charpentier, Marc Antoine, 1634–1704—Criticism and
interpretation.   I. Title.   II. Series.
ML410.C42H57 1990   782.1'092—dc20   89–16286
ISBN 0–19–316410–8 (Pbk.)
ISBN 0–19–316411–6

Set by Hope Services (Abingdon) Ltd
Printed in Great Britain by
Biddles Ltd., Guildford and King's Lynn

for Janet

PREFACE

WE have hardly begun to take the measure of Marc-Antoine Charpentier, even though, after two centuries of almost total neglect, the twentieth century has seen several waves of interest in him and his music, and his huge musical legacy—more than 550 compositions—is now acknowledged as one of the most treasurable of the Baroque era.

Around 1900, Michel Brenet and Henri Quittard were the first to rediscover Charpentier and signal his excellence. Only in 1945, however, did Claude Crussard write the first monograph on him—a brief work whose title declared Charpentier a 'musicien français oublié'. In the 1950s a number of scholars—mostly American—followed suit with dissertations and articles, and Guy-Lambert and others published a number of musical editions. Then, beginning in the late 1970s, the American keyboardist and conductor William Christie organized the early music ensemble Les Arts Florissants (its name borrowed from one of Charpentier's theatre pieces); it brought a new vitality and historical awareness to performances and recordings of Charpentier's music, and it was partly responsible for renewed efforts on the composer's behalf by a new group of younger French musicians and scholars. In the early 1980s my *catalogue raisonné* of Charpentier's works—*Les Œuvres de/The Works of Marc-Antoine Charpentier*—was published,[1] and a Société Marc-Antoine Charpentier was established in Paris; it has provided subsidies for various kinds of activities, including the first comprehensive monograph on the composer's life and works, Catherine Cessac's *Marc-Antoine Charpentier* (published in autumn 1988, shortly after the present book was written).

Yet, even if Charpentier's music has been increasingly admired, performed, recorded, published, and discussed in print, he himself remains a shadowy figure. We have no idea of his physical appearance, nor of his temperament or character.

---

[1] An index to the catalogue was published in H. W. Hitchcock, 'Marc-Antoine Charpentier: Mémoire and Index', *Recherches sur la musique classique française*, 23 (1985), 5–44.

(Surely we must discount the claim of the old Dassoucy, angry that Molière had turned to the younger composer as a collaborator, that Charpentier was 'un garçon [aux] ventricules du cerveau fort endommagés'.) Except for the fact that he was a Parisian, born almost certainly in 1643, we have no information about Charpentier's childhood or education prior to his going (for reasons that remain obscure) in the mid- or late 1660s to Rome, where he became a pupil of Giacomo Carissimi. There is hardly more than circumstantial and second-hand evidence about his movements thereafter, up to the date of his appointment as *maître de musique* at the Sainte-Chapelle du Palais in 1698, a half-dozen years before his death on 24 February 1704; even those years are short on facts and long on lacunae.

Apparently a bachelor, Charpentier seems to have left no legacy except his music, the manuscripts of which he bequeathed to a nephew who—fortunately for posterity—kept them virtually intact and ultimately sold them, in 1727, to the royal library. These 'mélanges autographes', now in the Bibliothèque Nationale at Paris (MS Rés. Vm^1 259; 28 vols.), contain around five hundred compositions; they are our principal source of Charpentier's music, for almost none was published during his lifetime, nor for about two hundred years thereafter.

This brief book on Charpentier's music, the first in English, begins with a sketch of Charpentier's career as a composer in Paris, to establish a context for my discussion of his works. The following chapters are organized according to a common seventeenth-century classification of music by destination: music for the church (*musique d'église*), music for the chamber (*musique de chambre*), and music for the theatre (*musique de théâtre*).

My work on this book, as on my other studies and editions of Charpentier's music, has been greatly facilitated by assistance from the personnel of a number of libraries—notably the New York Public Library, the Library of Congress, and especially the Départment de la Musique of the Bibliothèque Nationale at Paris, under its former Conservateur-en-chef, François Lesure. Marcelle Benoit has also been unfailingly supportive. I am most grateful to James R. Anthony and Paul C. Echols for their helpful comments on the manuscript, and in Hilary Walford I had a superb copy-editor; my dedication of the book bespeaks gratitude and appreciation of a more comprehensive sort.

H.W.H.

New York City
October 1989

CONTENTS

I
INTRODUCTION: CHARPENTIER IN PARIS

Musicus eram, inter bonis a bonis, et inter ignaros ab
ignaris nuncupatus. . . .

Charpentier, *Epitaphium Carpentarij*

CHARPENTIER was born in Paris in 1643 and apparently,
except for some years spent in Rome in the 1660s, lived and
worked there until his death on 24 February 1704. Although we
know nothing about his early years, and hardly more about those
he spent in Rome, we have considerable information about his
career as a composer in Paris (even if documentary evidence is
scanty).

According to the February 1681 issue of the invaluably
informative if gossipy *Mercure galant*, Charpentier was in Rome
for three years, as a pupil of Giacomo Carissimi (1605–74),
director of music at the Jesuits' German College and a highly
esteemed composer of church music, oratorios, and cantatas.
The young composer returned to Paris about 1670, to a musical
culture sharply divided between chauvinistic partisans of purely
French music—still smarting under the memory of Mazarin,
who before his death in 1661 had assiduously sought to
Italianize French musical culture by importing from Italy
impresarios, poets, singers, instrumentalists, stage architects,
and opera composers—and admirers of the progressive and
expressive Baroque music of *seicento* Italy. Ironically, 'purely
French' music was identified primarily with the *grands motets*
and the music for *ballets de cour, comédies-ballets*, and other stage
works of the Italian-born Jean-Baptiste Lully, while, for some,
the music of the Parisian Charpentier represented an excessive,
tasteless, Italianate adulteration of it. Nevertheless, he found
both adherents and admirers. Immediately upon his return from
Rome, some say, he became a protégé of the aristocratic Marie
de Lorraine, better known as 'Mademoiselle de Guise', a pious,
music-loving member of a distinguished family and heiress, as

of 1675, to its splendid *hôtel particulier* in the Marais.[1] Charpentier not only sang in her fine private musical ensemble —he was an *haute-contre*, that high natural tenor favoured by the French—but composed many works for it, until shortly before Mlle de Guise's death in 1688.

After the break-up in 1672 of the remarkable team of Molière and Lully—the latter having determined opportunistically to enter the field of opera composition—Molière turned to Charpentier as his new teammate. Their personal collaboration ended early in 1673 with Molière's death during the opening run of *Le Malade imaginaire*, but Charpentier continued until the mid-1680s to compose for the company, which came to be known as the Comédie-Française.

At the same time that he was gaining experience in composing theatre music, Charpentier was writing much sacred music. Indeed, his earliest extant manuscripts consist exclusively of religious works—mostly brief, small-scale ones (Tenebrae lessons and responses, small motets, settings of antiphons, canticles, and other liturgical texts) but also some lengthier ones for larger forces, including entire psalm settings and several Masses. The destination of these is unknown: no documentation has been found of commissions to Charpentier from any church or parish, or of his being employed by any, until very late in the 1670s. (The title of the *Salve Regina des Jésuites*, its manuscript datable in that decade, was added later, and by someone other than Charpentier.) The *Mercure galant* of September 1679 reported his having provided music on the feast of St Louis for a solemn Mass sponsored by the court artist Charles Le Brun for the parish of Saint-Hippolyte; and in April 1680 it recounted how, during Holy Week, crowds had gone to the Abbaye-aux-Bois to hear music by him. Five of his works of the 1680s and 1690s were composed for nuns of the convent of Port-Royal— not the Jansenist enclave (Port-Royal des Champs) but a second Port-Royal 'de Paris', in the Faubourg Saint-Jacques.

[1] Titon du Tillet, in his *Description du Parnasse françois* (Paris, 1727), was the first to claim that Mlle de Guise gave Charpentier lodging upon his return to Paris; Titon is supported in this opinion (but without precise documentation) by Patricia Ranum, 'A Sweet Servitude: A Musician's Life at the Court of Mlle de Guise', *Early Music*, 15 (1987), 347–60. But Charpentier's voluminous 'mélanges autographes' (*F-Pn* MS Rés. Vm¹ 259; 28 vols.), extraordinarily rich otherwise in informative details, offer no specific evidence that he was involved in the de Guise establishment before the 1680s. (*F-Pn* is the siglum for France-Paris nationale, the Bibliothèque Nationale at Paris, adopted by RISM, the Repertoire Internationale des Sources Musicales.)

By 1679 or 1680 Charpentier was in the service of the Grand Dauphin, especially as a composer of sacred works for the Dauphin's chapel. Louis XIV heard his music there and enjoyed it, reported the *Mercure galant*—not once, but twice (March 1681, May 1682). Possibly it was the Dauphin who commissioned Charpentier (or arranged for his being commissioned) to compose the music of two stage works on secular, courtly subjects, *Les Plaisirs de Versailles* and *La Fête de Rueil* of 1685, and possibly also the cantata *Orphée descendant aux enfers*.

In 1683 Louis XIV revamped the musical organization of the royal chapel; he retired the aged Henry Du Mont and Pierre Robert, who had been the principal *sous-maîtres* (music directors), and held a great contest to choose four new *sous-maîtres* to serve quarterly. Charpentier was one of thirty-five candidates who presented motets of their own composition at the King's Mass. Sixteen were chosen to compete in a second round, among them Charpentier; but, according to the *Mercure galant* (April 1683), he fell ill and had to withdraw from the competition. Two months later, however, the King awarded him a pension, either as a consolation prize or, as the *Mercure galant* (June 1683) implied, in gratitude for his services to the Dauphin. This was as close as Charpentier ever came to royal patronage, although in the early 1690s he was again on the periphery of court circles as teacher of music to Philippe d'Orléans, duc de Chartres, nephew of the King and future Regent of France. For him, according to Sébastien de Brossard—fellow-composer, admirer of Charpentier, and indefatigable music scholar and lexicographer—Charpentier wrote a brief treatise, *Règles de composition*, and apparently also the even briefer *Abrégé des règles de l'accompagnement*.

Although, as mentioned earlier, Charpentier composed many works for the musical establishment of Mlle de Guise during the 1680s (and perhaps earlier), he was not among those musicians who, upon her death in March 1688, received bequests under her will. This suggests that he had left her service earlier—perhaps because of the demands of another appointment, that of music director at the great Jesuit church of Saint-Louis (today Saint-Paul-Saint-Louis) in rue Saint-Antoine. Saint-Louis was noted for the extraordinary quality of its music: Le Cerf de la Viéville called it 'l'église de l'opéra', and Brossard termed its music directorship a 'poste alors des plus brillants'.[2] Thus, although composers like Lully and Michel-Richard de Lalande gained more *réclame* (and probably more income) as members of the royal musical establishment, Charpentier was not without stature and acclaim in Paris. The Jesuits sought him out for theatre music as well as for religious works: their Collège Louis-le-Grand was noted for its theatrical productions, including entire operas (to French librettos) that served as *intermèdes* to spoken dramas (in classical Greek or Latin), and in 1687 Charpentier composed the music for one such opera, *Celse Martyr*; on 25 February 1688 the college presented another *tragédie en musique* by him, *David et Jonathas*, which had a considerable success both in Paris and in provincial productions. These were full-scale works, each in a prologue and five acts: one historian of Jesuit theatre remarked of *Celse martyr*, 'One might say that it was rather the three acts of the Latin play that served as *intermèdes* to the French one.'[3]

Lully died in 1687, leaving the path open to productions of works by other composers at the Académie Royale de Musique —the Opéra. In 1693 Charpentier's theatrical masterpiece, the tragedy *Médée*, was mounted there. (Its libretto was by a longtime collaborator, Thomas Corneille, younger brother of the more famous playwright Pierre.) Predictably, in view of the continued presence on the Parisian musical scene of un-compromising partisans of Lully's stage works, *Médée* was not too well received and had only ten performances. Nevertheless, Charpentier's noble supporters, the duc de Chartres and the Dauphin, attended more than once; the King accepted the dedication of the work with the remark that he knew Charpentier to be 'un homme habile'; and the firm of Ballard, which had long enjoyed a royal monopoly on music publishing in Paris, brought out a full score in 1694. (This was the only such publication Charpentier enjoyed in his lifetime, though in 1676

[2] Le Cerf de la Viéville, *Comparaison de la musique italienne et de la musique française* (Brussels, 1704–6; repr. Geneva, 1972); 2nd edn. in Pierre Bourdelot and Jacques Bonnet, *Histoire de la musique et de ses effets* (Amsterdám, 1725; repr. Graz, 1966), iv. 163; Sébastien de Brossard, 'Catalogue des livres de musique . . . qui sont dans le cabinet du Sʳ Sebastien de Brossard . . .' (*F-Pn* MS Rés. Vm⁸ 21, fo. 226.

[3] 'L'on peut dire que c'était plutôt la pièce latine en trois actes qui servait d'intermèdes à la pièce française' (Ernest Boysse, *Le Théâtre des Jésuites* (Paris, 1880), 193; quoted in Robert W. Lowe, *Marc-Antoine Charpentier et l'opéra de collège* (Paris, 1966), 52).

Ballard had issued a small collection of theatre music by him (*Airs de la comédie de Circé*), and a few other *airs* appeared in the *Mercure galant*.)

Charpentier's final post was as *maître de musique* at the Sainte-Chapelle du Palais, to which he was named on 18 June 1698, succeeding the recently deceased François Chaperon. Whether or not the duc de Chartres had interceded on behalf of his former teacher to obtain the appointment for him, as Brossard claimed, Charpentier was an apt choice, and he concluded his career with a series of major compositions for that small but important church. Perhaps also a product of the Sainte-Chapelle years is the very curious cantata *Epitaphium Carpentarij*, in which the shade of Charpentier (assigned, certainly not by coincidence, to an *haute-contre*) counsels two friends and describes the music in heaven. He also assesses ruefully his own status as a French musician, in the sentence that serves as epigraph for this chapter: 'I was a musician, thought to be among the good ones by the good, and among the ignorant ones by the ignorant. . . .'[4] Perhaps a more balanced opinion was the posthumous one of the *Journal de Trévoux*, which, taking notice in 1709 of a slim volume of *petits motets* by Charpentier just published by his nephew and inheritor, spoke of the composer as 'un des plus excellents musiciens que la France ait eus' and emphasized his

rare talent for expressing in music the sense of the words, and for moving [the listener]. Thousands here in Paris still recall what a great impression his music made, a far cry from that which is admirable only for its sonorous beauty, without relating to the text—and even farther from that which appeals only by being bizarre. It is true [however] that Mr Charpentier, who was second to none in Latin [i.e. sacred] music, did not succeed so well in French [i.e. secular].[5]

[4] See also Ch. 4 n. 6.
[5] 'Edouard a imprimé des motets de feu Mr Charpentier, un des plus excellents musiciens que la France ait eus. Il était l'élève du Carissimi. C'est sous ce grand maître qu'il avait acquis le talent si rare d'exprimer par les tons de la musique le sens des paroles, et de toucher. Mille gens se souviennent encore à Paris du grand effet que produisait sa musique, bien différente de celle qui ne se fait admirer que par la beauté d'une harmonie qui n'a aucun rapport aux paroles, plus différente de celle dont la bizarrerie fait tout le prix. Il est vrai que Mr Charpentier, qui n'a cédé à personne dans la musique latine, n'a pas réussi également dans la musique française' (quoted in Michel Brenet, 'La Librairie musicale en France de 1653 à 1790, d'après les Registres de privilèges', *Sammelbände der internationalen Musikgesellschaft*, viii (1906–7), 401–66).

Brossard, on the other hand, emphasized Charpentier's profound musical knowledge and compositional skill in general: 'He has always been considered by all the real connoisseurs as the most profound and learned of modern musicians.'[6] Of *Médée*, among the most 'French' of his *musique française*, Brossard wrote, 'It is unquestionably the most expert and exquisite of all those [operas] that have been published, at least since the death of Mr de Lully, [and] the one, more than all other operas without exception, from which may be learned the essentials of good composition.'[7]

---

[6] 'Il a toujours passé au goût de tous les vrais connoisseurs pour le plus profond et le plus sçavant des musiciens modernes' ('Catalogue', fo. 226).

[7] 'Il est sans contredit le plus sçavant et le plus recherché de tous ceux qui ont été imprimés, du moins depuis la mort de Mr de Lully, [et] celui de tous les Opéras, sans exception, dans lequel on peut apprendre plus de choses essentielles à la bonne composition' ('Catalogue', fo. 227–8).

II
MUSIC FOR THE CHURCH I:
THE LITURGICAL WORKS AND
PSALM SETTINGS

> La musique est un mélange harmonieux des sons aigus,
> moyens, et graves. . . . La seule diversité en fait toute la
> perfection.
>
> Charpentier, *Règles de composition*

ALTHOUGH Charpentier wrote a considerable amount of
secular music, especially for the theatre, he was primarily a
composer of music for the church, and we have many more
religious works by him than works of any other type. The legacy
of his sacred music is summarized in Table 1.[1]

As is apparent, the number of Charpentier's sacred compositions alone reaches almost five hundred—far too many,
obviously, to discuss in any but the most selective way in a book
as brief as this one. I shall consider this repertoire in two
chapters—the liturgical works and psalm settings in the present
one, the motets and instrumental works in the next.

What I should like to emphasize above all in these chapters is
the *diversity* of Charpentier's works in virtually every genre.
Diversity was for him the source of all perfection in music (as
this chapter's epigraph reveals), and his music reflects that
aesthetic very clearly—partly, to be sure, because of the diverse
kinds and levels of patronage he enjoyed. But diversity of all
kinds is apparent in the works themselves—in their dimensions,
the performance resources they require, their interplay of vocal
and instrumental forces, their metrical and rhythmic organization,

---

[1] This summary and others to follow are based on H. W. Hitchcock, *Les œuvres de/The
Works of Marc-Antoine Charpentier: Catalogue raisonné* (Paris, 1982), which is abstracted
in the works-list appended to the article on Charpentier in *The New Grove* (repr. with a
few revisions in *The New Grove French Baroque Masters* (London, 1986), 89–112).
Citations herein of 'Cat.' numbers refer to this source.

TABLE I. *A summary of Charpentier's religious music*

	No. of works	Cat. numbers
I Vocal works		
A Mass settings	11	1–11
B Other liturgical works		
1 Sequences	4	12–15
2 Antiphons	37	16–52
3 Hymns	19	53–71
4 Magnificat settings	10	72–81
5 Litany of Loreto settings	9	82–90
6 Tenebrae lessons and responses	54	91–144
7 Te Deum settings	4	145–8
C Psalm settings	84	149–232
D Motets		
1 Elevation motets	48	233–80
2 'Domine salvum' motets	25	281–305
3 Occasional motets	85	306–90
4 Dramatic motets ('oratorios')	35	391–425
5 Miscellaneous motets	14	426–39
II Instrumental works	32	508–39

their textures, their treatment of text, their formal designs and structures.

Much has been made of Charpentier's Italian training and thus his 'Italianate' music; much was made of this, in a polemical way, during his lifetime. I shall be at pains, however, to emphasize his mastery of French traditions and idioms as well as his debt to Italian models—thus, to insist on the diversity of his stylistic tendencies—and in fact shall suggest that not the least of his achievements was a synthesis of Italian and French styles presaging without ostentation the 'goûts réunis' on which such later composers as François Couperin prided themselves.

Mass Settings

Charpentier's Mass settings—eleven for voices and instruments, one for instruments alone, and all very different—make a fine beginning to our consideration of his music's diversity and breadth of stylistic range. That he wrote as many Masses as he did reflects the fact that he was not a composer for the royal chapel. Louis XIV attended Mass daily but preferred a Low Mass spoken by the celebrant, not a High Mass chanted and sung by clergy and choir. Thus, the composers for the royal chapel in the age of the Sun King had no reason to compose settings of the Mass Ordinary—Kyrie, Gloria, Credo, Sanctus/Benedictus, and Agnus Dei—of the sort written in the hundreds in earlier times, and we have no such Mass settings by the major chapel composers such as Du Mont, Robert, Lully, and Lalande. The chapel musicians did, however, perform three motets during the course of the royal Mass: a substantial *grand motet*, in several movements, which was to conclude before the elevation of the host; a briefer *petit motet* on a eucharistic text, performed at the elevation of the host; and, at the end of the Mass, a 'Domine salvum' motet—a choral prayer for the King's good health, its text Verse 10 of Psalm 19: *Domine salvum fac regem, et exaudi nos in die qua invocaverimus te* ('O Lord, save the king, and hear us in the hour when we call upon thee'). These conventions of the King's Mass explain why, reflecting the absolutist atmosphere of late-seventeenth-century Paris, most of Charpentier's Masses include—as integral components along with Ordinary items—either an elevation motet interpolated, in the Sanctus movement, between the first 'Hosanna in excelsis' and the 'Benedictus qui venit', or a 'Domine salvum' setting following the Agnus Dei, or both.

Charpentier's Mass settings are diverse in various ways.

The earliest Mass (untitled in the manuscript source) calls for very modest resources: four voices (SATB), two violins (or perhaps recorders: the instrumentation is not specified, and no idiomatic traits point to one type of instrument over the other), and basso continuo. At the opposite pole is the immense contemporaneous *Messe à quatre chœurs* for twelve soloists, four choirs (each SATB), doubling strings, and four continuo groups, each with its own organ. This is very much in the polychoral Italian style—not that of Venice and Gabrieli or Monteverdi, but that of Rome and the 'colossal Baroque' sacred works of Benevoli or Pitoni. It is instructive to compare Charpentier's four-choir Mass with the copy which he made (with marginal comments and additional 'Remarques sur les messes à 16 parties d'Italie') of the *Missa Mirabiles elationes a maris a 16*—also for four choirs of four parts each—by the

9

Roman maestro Francesco Beretta, and to see how closely it conforms to such Roman models.

French sacred music had for some decades featured contrast between a *petit chœur* of vocal soloists and a *grand chœur* or *tous* (tutti) of choristers, and similarly between a concertino-like instrumental *petit chœur* versus an orchestral *grand chœur*. To this tradition belong Charpentier's *Messe pour les trépassés à 8* and the *Messe à 8 voix et 8 violons et flûtes*, both for double chorus, soloists, and orchestra of strings and recorders. The Mass for the Dead includes an elevation motet ('Pie Jesu') in addition to Kyrie, Sanctus/Benedictus, and Agnus Dei movements, and together with it another motet is also to be performed—a 'Motet for the Dead' subtitled *Plainte des âmes du purgatoire*. As such, this Mass for All Souls' Day is the most elaborate of its type to have been composed. The *Messe à 8 voix . . .*, like several others of Charpentier's Masses, calls for organ or orchestral versets to be added in *alternatim* fashion to the material composed by Charpentier. Following the opening Kyrie movement, for example, the composer writes in the manuscript, 'Here the organ may play a verset, or if there is no organ some symphony must be played'[2]—'symphony' in this context meaning simply an orchestral movement.

Unique is the *Messe pour le Port Royal*, not only in being scored for women's voices (three soprano soloists and unison soprano chorus, plus *basse continue*) but in including various items of the Mass Proper—Introit, Gradual, Offertory, Communion—and in fact two of each, one 'pour Ste Marguerite' and one 'pour St François'. Unique in a different way is the charming *Messe de minuit à 4 voix, flûtes et violons, pour Noël*, composed for the midnight Mass at Christmas. Much of its music is based on the tunes of traditional, popular French *noëls* (Christmas carols). The opening Kyrie, for example, is wholly based on the bourrée-related tune of 'Joseph est bien marié', the Gloria partially on the skipping melody of 'Les Bourgeois de Châtre'. Even portions of the solemn Credo text are set to *noëls* ('Vous qui désirez sans fin', 'Voici le jour solennel de Noël', and 'A la venue de Noël'), though its most serious moment—the statements of Christ's incarnation, his mortal existence, and his death under Pontius Pilate—is given wholly original music, and

---

[2] 'Ici l'orgue joue un couplet si l'on veut, ou s'il n'y a point d'orgue il faudra jouer quelque symphonie.'

appropriately sober. The prayerful Agnus Dei, on the other hand, is somewhat surprisingly set in *alternatim* fashion to the jolly minuet melody of 'À minuit fut fait un réveil', the choir singing only the second of the three liturgical invocations, the first being an orchestral verset (based on the *noël* tune) which is repeated as the third (Ex. 1).[3]

The ripest and richest among Charpentier's Masses is *Assumpta est Maria: Missa sex vocibus cum simphonia* (1699?) for soloists, six-part chorus, recorders, strings, and continuo. Charpentier's reputation as a 'learned' musician—'profond et sçavant', said Brossard—was based partly on his secure mastery of imitative counterpoint, which is striking in such passages of this Mass as the grave Kyrie, various solo trios in the Credo movement, and perhaps especially the ebullient opening of the Sanctus (Ex. 2).

The *Messe pour plusieurs instruments au lieu des orgues*—a unique example of an orchestral Mass by a seventeenth-century French composer—is unusual in other ways as well. It will be considered in my discussion of the sacred instrumental works in Chapter 3.

Other Liturgical Works

Although the Masses by Charpentier do not draw on plainchant for their themes (at least the Ordinary movements do not), a number of his other liturgical compositions begin, at least, with chant-derived themes—a gesture to tradition suggesting the general conservatism of French seventeenth-century sacred music (apart from the special 'official' style of the *grands motets* that had crystallized in the royal chapel). Thus the massive *Prose des morts*—one of four settings of sequences by Charpentier—opens with the familiar Gregorian 'Dies irae' melody, and two thematically related settings of the Marian antiphon 'Salve regina'—one for three solo voices, the other for three choirs—both commence with a point of imitation on a theme derived from the opening of the chant melody, as does also another Marian antiphon, 'Regina coeli'. Among the nineteen hymns, too, several are chant-based—including settings of the ancient poems 'Pange lingua gloriosi' and 'Iste Confessor Domini'. A

---

[3] Unless otherwise indicated, music examples are drawn from Charpentier's 'mélanges autographes' (*F-Pn* MS Rés. Vm[1] 259; 28 vols.).

Ex. 1. *Messe de minuit* (Cat. 9), Agnus Dei (xxv. 76ᵛ–77)

Second Agnus Dei

* Troisième Agnus [:] Reprenez la simphonie
de devant l'Agnus Dei.

[Dal segno
℈ alla Fine]*

number of the Tenebrae compositions also begin with melodies whose general contour, if not their arabesque-like detail, echo the Gregorian formulae for reciting the lessons. Several of the ten Magnificat settings similarly open with references to plainsong Magnificat 'tones'. Particularly conservative, almost peculiarly so, are three hymns in honour of St Nicasius of Rouen: not only are they for unaccompanied male voice; they are chant-like in style and written in square black notation. A few others of the liturgical works are also without accompaniment, though they are not at all chant-like and are written in modern notation; among these are the charming *Antiphona sine organo ad Virginem* ('Sub tuum praesidium') and the delicate *Iste Confessor*,

Ex. 2. *[Missa] Assumpta est Maria* (Cat. 11), Sanctus, opening (xxvii. 13)

both of a purity of line and delicacy of texture reminiscent of
Renaissance polyphony.

A religiously utilitarian conservatism lies behind some of
Charpentier's church works, those composed in sets reflecting
liturgical cycles. Notable among these are a set of three
antiphons to be sung after the first, third, and fifth psalms of a
Vespers Office of a Confessor not Pontiff; a set composed on
each of the seven 'O-Antiphons' of Advent; a very fine set on the
four Marian antiphons of the Office of Compline, one for each
quarter of the year ('Alma redemptoris mater', 'Ave regina
coelorum', 'Regina coeli', and 'Salve regina'); and a number of
sets of Tenebrae lessons and responsories.

By contrast to such traditionalism, Charpentier is not averse to the most startling modernisms (from the French point of view), especially of harmony but also of design and structure. The antiphon text of the *Salve Regina à trois chœurs* falls naturally into three sections, which Charpentier punctiliously observes in his setting. The text of the middle section is differentiated from the outer ones by being extremely personal: it turns to the first person, and the speakers identify themselves as 'exiles, children of Eve . . . groaning and weeping in this vale of tears'. Charpentier sets this section for his third 'choir'—actually three soloists, in a combination particularly favoured by him (*haute-contre*, tenor, bass)—with a hair-raisingly chromatic depiction of the agonized text.[4] One is reminded of the frequent comments, for and against Charpentier's harmonic language, that appeared during his life and shortly thereafter. Serré des Rieux lauded it:

Charpentier revêtu d'une sage richesse,
Des Chromatiques Sons fit sentir la finesse:
Dans la belle Harmonie il s'ouvrit un chemin,
Neuvièmes et Tritons brillèrent sous sa main.[5]

For another compatriot, however, Charpentier's Italianate chromaticism was too much:

Si l'on croit Charpentier, il a fait des merveilles,
Mais quels tristes accords écorchent nos oreilles!
Pour composer un chant si beau,
Sans doute dans ce jour quelque maudit corbeau
Aura meslé sa voix à celle de Corneille!

Yet another put it even more bluntly: 'Charpentier est barbare . . .'[6]

One exceptionally unusual work, in fact apparently unique in Renaissance or Baroque music, is the set of pieces on the seven 'Great Antiphons' sung with the Magnificat at Vespers during the last week of Advent. The text of each begins with the exclamation 'O'—'O sapientia . . .', 'O Adonai . . .', 'O radix

---

[4] Excerpts from this section, and parallel ones from a *petit motet* (Cat. 23) on the same text, are reproduced in James Anthony, *French Baroque Music from Beaujoyeulx to Rameau* (rev. edn., New York: W. W. Norton; London: B. T. Batsford, Ltd., 1978), 190–1.

[5] *Les Dons des enfants de Latone* (1734), quoted in Lowe, *Charpentier et l'opéra de collège*, p. 15.

[6] The two last opinions—from *Chansonnier Clerambault*, ix. 81, and *Recueil de chansons anecdotes*, vi. 271 (1702), respectively—are quoted in Pierre Mélèse, *Répertoire analytique des documents contemporains d'information et de critique concernant le théâtre à Paris sous Louis XIV, 1659–1715* (Paris, 1934), 196, 69.

Jesse . . .', etc.—and thus they are often termed the O-Antiphons. They explore various Advent themes, and each antiphon underlines its particular theme with an entreaty, to the representative of the Deity addressed, to 'come'—'come and teach us the way of understanding', 'come and deliver us with your strong arm', 'come and deliver us, do not tarry', and so on. Charpentier precedes his music for the seven antiphons with a setting of the eucharistic 'O salutaris hostia' and titles the whole set *Salut de la veille des O et les 7 O suivant le romain* ('Greeting on the Eve of the O[-Antiphons] and the Seven O[-Antiphons] according to the Roman [Rite]'). His settings are varied, some inviting performance by solo voices (mostly the trio of *haute-contre*, tenor, and bass), some requiring chorus as well; some accompanied only by continuo, some calling for obbligato instruments or even orchestra. Most interestingly, the antiphon set is flanked in the manuscript by two groups of instrumental *noëls*, and marginal notes make it clear that these are to be performed along with the O-Antiphons, lending a Christmastide note of popularesque jubilation to the Advent Vespers services.

Among the Magnificat settings is one extraordinary one—for the same male trio that figures in the pieces just discussed, plus two violins and continuo—which is based throughout its entire 357 bars on the falling-tetrachord bass ostinato G–F–Eb–D, 'répétée 89 fois', as Charpentier remarks in the manuscript (perhaps with pride, but perhaps just as a cautionary note to a copyist). Few pieces by him reveal as clearly his thoroughgoing absorption of mid-century Italian modes of musical planning and expression as this one, with its two-violin ritornellos punctuating the ends of verses, its exuberant melismata on such phrases as 'et exultavit spiritus meus', 'beatam me dicent omnes generationes', and 'Gloria Patri et Filio', and most especially its cunning overriding, by the most ingeniously varied vocal phrases, of the inexorably revolving bass ostinato. One is reminded of such late works of Monteverdi as the *Lamento della ninfa* in the Eighth Book of madrigals or *Zefiro torna* in the Ninth.

In contrast to this few-voiced, Italianate Magnificat setting is the *Magnificat à 8 voix et 8 instruments*, dating from the early 1680s and most probably composed either for the chapel of the Dauphin or for the Jesuits. (The single singer named in the manuscript is 'Mr Dun', a frequent bass soloist at the church of Saint-Louis.) This is not only the mightiest of Charpentier's

Magnificats but is planned very much in the manner of an 'official' courtly *grand motet*, of the sort defined in the 1660s by Lully, elaborated by Du Mont and Robert into the 1680s, and given its highest expression by Lalande (whose motets were published only posthumously, in 1729). Charpentier's *Magnificat* calls for six vocal soloists, double chorus (SATB/SATB), double orchestra (each orchestra made up of strings, recorders,[7] oboes, and bassoons), and continuo group. Its design is as shown in Table 2 (the movement numbers not original). The arch-like symmetry of this design is striking; it is not unusual in Charpentier's multi-movement works. The pillars of the arch are the first, central, and last movements (1, 4, 7), which are scored for the entire complex, are the longest movements of the work, and are roughly the same in length. The other movements, shorter and slighter (*petit-chœur* movements, we might appropriately call them), form pairs flanking the central pillar; movements 2 and 5 are for solo voices (with different pairs of obbligato instruments), 3 and 6 for trios. Some sense of the grandeur of this work can perhaps be had from the opening of the vocal entries of No. 1 (Ex. 3*b*), following the Prelude; the solo *haute-contre*'s intonation of 'Magnificat anima mea Dominum' is derived, as shown, from the Gregorian Magnificat Tone I (ending D) (Ex. 3*a*).

TABLE 2. *The design of the* Magnificat à 8 voix et 8 instruments

Section	Scoring	Bars
1. Prelude/Magnificat	Double orch./*Tous*	84
2. Quia fecit	S solo; 2 fls., b.c.	26
3. Et misericordia ejus	ATB trio; b.c.	29
4. Fecit potentiam	*Tous*	100
5. Suscepit Israel	S solo; 2 vns., b.c.	38
6. Sicut locutus est	ATB trio; b.c.	26
7. Gloria Patri	*Tous* with B solo	72
		375

Ex. 3*a*. Gregorian Magnificat Tone I (ending D)

[7] Charpentier consistently cites 'flûtes d'allemagne' or 'flûtes allemandes' when he wishes transverse flutes; the simple word 'flûtes', as in the manuscript of this work (elsewhere, occasionally, 'flûtes douces'), indicates recorders.

18

Ex. 3*b*. *Magnificat à 8 voix* . . . (Cat. 74)., bars 23–48 (xi. 4ᵛ)

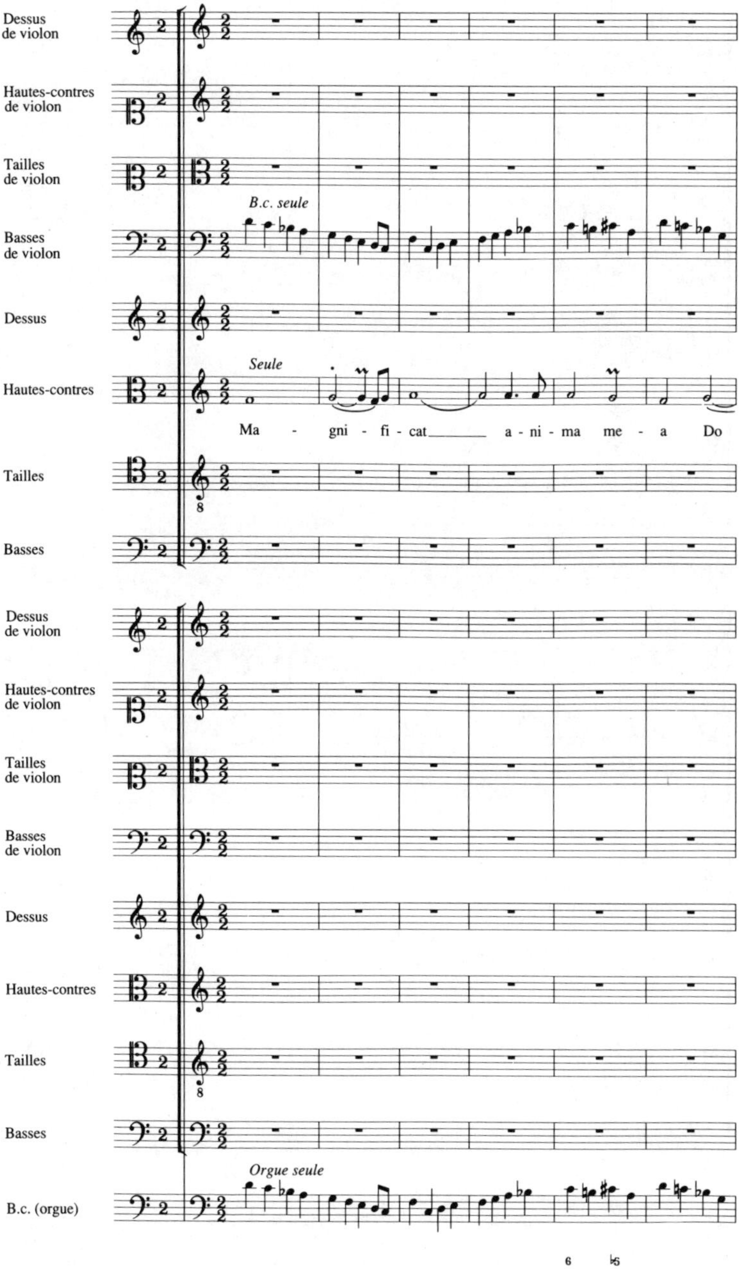

21

8. Aria 1 (*da cape*

Among Charpentier's most original and influential groups of sacred compositions are his Tenebrae lessons and responsories.[8] These were composed for those very special Offices of Matins on Maundy Thursday, Good Friday, and Holy Saturday in Holy Week which take their nickname from the gradual extinction during them of the lights in the church. (In Charpentier's time, Tenebrae services were celebrated not in the morning, as is implicit in the very term 'Matins', but the evening before; thus he titles Thursday's lessons as for 'Mercredi saint', Friday's as for 'Jeudi saint', and Saturday's as for 'Vendredi saint'.) The lessons are rooted, in part, in the traditional Gregorian 'tonus lamentationis' but even more deeply in the vocal style of the *airs de cour*—especially their highly ornamented *doubles*—of Antoine Boësset, Jean-Baptiste Boësset, and Michel Lambert. The first of Lambert's two cycles of Tenebrae lessons, thought to date from the early 1660s, may have influenced Charpentier; on the other hand, the latter's own lessons and responsories—more carefully composed, leaving nothing to improvisation (as do Lambert's)—seem to have influenced Lambert's second cycle (1689) and initiated a distinctive style of French Tenebrae music—a style termed by René Jacobs (after Käser) the 'high melismatic style' and best known in François Couperin's well-known set of lessons.[9]

What is remarkable about Charpentier's first Tenebrae pieces (Cat. 91–5)—probably the earliest music by him that has come down to us—is that they seem thoroughly French, hardly touched by the Italian idioms apparent in so much of his other early music and with which he was identified in the politicized musical atmosphere of Paris after Mazarin's death. Later lessons are more tinged with Italianisms, more relaxed and expansively lyrical, and also firmer in tonality, more confident in counterpoint; and, though they reveal a typically French respect for careful textual declamation in basically syllabic style, they often blossom out into melismata—not only the exuberant vocalises which set in high relief the Hebrew letters introducing each verse, but affective, Italianate word-painting at other

[8] The former are treated in detail in Theodor Käser, *Die Leçon de Ténèbres im 17. und 18. Jahrhundert* (Bern, 1966).
[9] See Jacobs's excellent essay accompanying the recording by Concerto Vocale of nine Tenebrae compositions by Charpentier (Harmonia Mundi France HM 1005/6/7; recorded in August 1977 and January 1978).

23

moments. Typical is the glorious phrase shown in Example 4, to the last clause of the agonized text '[He hath enclosed my ways with hewn stone;] he hath made my paths crooked'; this is from a small cycle of the late 1680s (Cat. 123–5) setting the third lesson of each day, for a low tenor (*basse-taille*) with two flutes and two violins. The text of every Tenebrae lesson ends the same way, with the stern injunction *Jerusalem, Jerusalem, convertere ad Dominum Deum tuum* ('Jerusalem, Jerusalem, turn back to the Lord your God'), and in this cycle of lessons Charpentier underscores these refrains by using the same music for each, thus powerfully unifying the group of pieces; this is also true of virtually every other set by him.

Charpentier later essayed even larger Tenebrae cycles: he composed as a unit, with various alternative passages and ritornellos, *Les Neuf Leçons de ténèbres*—the entire group of nine

Ex. 4. *Troisième leçon de ténèbres du Jeudi saint pour une basse-taille avec 2 flûtes et 2 violons* (Cat. 124), bars 251–60 (xxiii. 22)

lessons (three for each day); and he made one game attempt to set *Les Neufs Répons de chaque jour*—twenty-seven responsories in all—but gave up in frustration, after completing only nine, 'à cause du changement du bréviaire' (as he notes in the manuscript of the *Neuvième répons après la troisième leçon du troisième nocturne du Mercredi saint*, referring to changes in the Paris ritual made in 1680). There are some especially beautiful later responsories—which tend in general to be less extravagantly ornamented, more cantabile in vocal line, than the lessons— notably a 'Tenebrae factae sunt' for bass soloist (the *basse chantante* so prized by the French), recorders, strings, and continuo; a poignant 'O vos omnes' for solo soprano, two recorders, and continuo; and a chromatically coloured 'Omnes amici mei' for high tenor (*haute-taille*), two recorders, and continuo.

Only four settings by Charpentier of the Te Deum have survived, although we know he composed at least six. Two of these are of especially impressive dimensions, each more than seven hundred bars long and demanding very elaborate performance forces: the *Te Deum à 8 voix avec flûtes et violons*, an early work of uncertain destination, in C major (a 'gai et guerrier' key, according to Charpentier),[10] and an even more powerful Te Deum in D of the early 1690s (Cat. 146) scored for eight soloists, SATB chorus, woodwinds, trumpets, timpani,

[10] In his *Règles de composition* he systematically outlines the basic affects of a remarkably broad range of keys, in both major and minor modes (C, D, Eb, E, F, G, A, Bb, and B)—apparently the first such list of 'key feelings' (*énergie des modes* is Charpentier's term). The entire list is reproduced in *L'Avant-scène opéra*, 68 (Oct. 1984), 98–9, and (in translation) in H. W. Hitchcock, 'The Latin Oratorios of Marc-Antoine Charpentier', *Musical Quarterly*, 41 (1955), 41–65, and Anthony, *French Baroque Music*, p. 189).

and strings. This orchestra had been established at court by Lully—borrowing winds, trumpets, and drums from the Grande Écurie, to add to the *vingt-quatre violons du Roi*—for works of special celebratory éclat. The D major Te Deum is in the 'joyeux et très guerrier' key (Charpentier's characterization) favoured by French composers for settings of the jubilant Te Deum text, which in the *grand siècle* inevitably made a musical appearance at moments of national elation such as military victories, recovery from illness of the King, birth of a royal heir, and such. This Te Deum is especially well known through recordings (the first of which helped to spark the Charpentier revival of the 1950s); and its prelude—an infectious Marche en

Ex. 5. Te Deum in D (Cat. 146), conclusion (bars 699–720) (x. 85)

rondeau in A b A c A form—is universally known in Europe as the theme music of Eurovision productions. Few works by Charpentier have as blazingly climactic a conclusion, with its powerful stomping rhythms, its militant, fanfare-like ritornellos, and its affirmative declaration of God's never-ending support of true believers ('In te Domini speravi, non confundar in aeternum'): Charpentier stretches out 'in aeternum' in long-held notes serenely secure amidst the tumult of the accompanying counterpoint (Ex. 5).

Psalm Settings

As the outline of Charpentier's sacred compositions earlier in this chapter shows, we have eighty-four settings of complete psalms by him (including the conclusion of a lost Psalm 129). About half of these conclude with the Lesser Doxology ('Gloria Patri et Filio et Spiritui Sancto . . . in saecula saeculorum. Amen.'), indicating their intended use as liturgical items of Office services (mostly Vespers). The others were also, however, intended for performance during worship services, though as decorative 'motet-psalms' (as we might call them); these served, precisely like other motets of the time, as paraliturgical additions to a Mass or an Office, their texts often related to the religious theme of the day but not part of the authorized liturgy. These two groups of Charpentier's psalm settings are stylistically indistinguishable; thus it would be pedantic to separate the liturgical psalms from those without the 'Gloria Patri', and here I shall consider them together.[11]

Charpentier's liturgical psalm settings may be itemized as follows, italicized numbers indicating those psalms set more than once (and the number of such settings enclosed in parentheses): Psalms 4, 5,[12] 19, *109* (6), *110* (4), *111* (5), *112* (2), 115, *116* (6), 121, 125, *126* (3), 131, *147* (3)—a total of 14 psalms in 36 settings. In addition, there are 8 settings of Psalm 129 with two added verses ('Requiem aeternam dona eis

[11] It must be said, however, that no one has made a close study of Charpentier's psalms, especially in the context of the Paris ritual of his time. Perhaps a future scholar will prove my treatment of the liturgical psalms and the motet-psalms together to have been incorrect.

[12] This is the number Charpentier consistently assigns to 'Quare fremuerunt gentes', Psalm 2 in the Vulgate.

Domine. Et lux perpetua luceat eis.') as at Vespers of the Office for the Dead; and as mentioned, for a composition of Psalm 129 that has not survived, a setting of the doxology alone: *Gloria Patri pour le De profundis en C sol ut bémol à quatre voix, 4 violons et flûtes.* Thus the total number of liturgical psalm settings is 44. The motet-psalms may be itemized similarly as follows: Psalms 1, 3, 5, 8, 12, 15, *19* (3), 20, 26, 34, 41, 45, 46, *50* (4), 62, 67, *75* (2), *83* (2), 84, 86, 87, *91* (2), 97, 99, 107, 121, 123, 126, 127, 136, 148—a total of 31 psalms in 39 settings. Thus, all told, we have, as noted, 83 psalm settings by Charpentier (plus the lone *Gloria Patri . . .*). They span virtually his entire creative career, from about 1670 ('Laudate pueri Dominum') to about 1700, the latest precisely datable examples being the three Psalms for Holy Week 1699. That being so, my approach to a selective consideration of them can differ somewhat from that of the first half of this chapter: though still emphasizing the diversity of Charpentier's works, I shall also attempt to suggest the chronological development of his sacred-music style.

Most striking is the rapidity of that development. If my datings of Charpentier's manuscripts are valid, within a short decade—basically that of the 1670s—his music moved from a fairly tentative, lacklustre, and almost wholly Italianate style (except for those early Tenebrae pieces) to one of confident assurance, colourfulness, and originality, with elements of French tradition absorbed and joined to those from Italy.

The earliest psalm settings (Cat. 149–55) are all scored for SATB chorus (from which soloists are drawn) with two treble obbligato instruments (presumably violins, though recorders would be perfectly appropriate, the instrumental writing not being particularly idiomatic for strings), and *basse continue*. The text settings are not very subtle or sensitive: Italianate melismata abound, and their relevance to the text is not always clear; Italianate upbeat phrase-beginnings often threaten textual coherence, as in Example 6, the beginning of the 'Gloria Patri' of one setting of Psalm 111 (Cat. 154). There are many passages of self-consciously 'learnèd' imitative counterpoint, virtually in a retrospective (and one might almost say 'Roman') *stile antico*, since the continuo is hardly more than a *basse seguente* doubling the lowest voice part. A second group of psalms, however, datable from only a bit later in the 1670s (Cat. 158, 160–2), climaxes with the splendid *Exaudiat à 8 voix, flûtes et violons*, a

Ex. 6. [*Psalm III*] (Cat. 154), bars 197–200 (xiv. 28)

massive, self-assured setting of Psalm 19 for soloists, double chorus, and double orchestra of winds and strings that is almost six hundred bars long. It is contemporaneous with the equally impressive C major Te Deum (Cat. 145) for similar forces (and of even greater length). Both resonate with regal éclat; both may have been written for the church of Saint-Louis on the occasion of some triumph of Louis XIV.

Another group of psalm settings unified by their scoring (Cat. 170–9, 181, 185–8) extends from the late 1670s into the mid-1680s. These are works of *petit-motet* dimensions, for trios of solo voices—mostly two sopranos and bass—with two treble instruments and continuo. The series begins with a 'Super flumina [Psalm 136] des demoiselles Pièches'—a reference to the sisters Magdaleine and Marguerite Pièche, well-known

31

sopranos, who with three other members of their family performed in the chapel ensemble of the Grand Dauphin. They are mentioned in others of this group of few-voice settings, which thus may have been composed for the Dauphin's chapel. These are very confident and competent works, with many niceties of text expression and touches of originality. The setting of Psalm 136 just cited opens with a chromatic setting of the lamenting text, full of intense suspension-dissonances and with a remarkable breadth of line and accuracy of declamation (Ex. 7a). At an opposite pole is the astonishing projection of jubilation (at the very word 'Jubilate') in a setting of Psalm 97; this is achieved through ascending melodic lines, in ascending imitative entries, in sequences that rise by step (Ex. 7b).

Ex. 7a. *Psalmus David [136ᵘˢ] centesimus trigesimus sextus: Super flumina Babylonis* (Cat. 170), bars 27–46 (iii. 93)

Ex. 7*b*. [*Psalm 97*] (Cat. 176), bars 66–77 (xix. 20ᵛ)

(Rejoice in God, all ye on earth.)

Other subtleties on behalf of vivid projection of textual
meaning make their appearance in this group of psalms:
expressive and dramatic use of rests and indications for pauses
between sections ('Faites ici une petite pause'); increased
richness of harmony; nuances of tempo, such as a differentiation
between ₵ ('vite') and 2 ('plus lent') time signatures, an
indication (with no change of metre) that a passage should be
taken 'Lentement jusqu'à la fin du couplet' or that another, in a
section all in C metre, is suddenly to be taken 'à 4 temps gais';
ending a work with a *petite reprise*—repetition of the last phrase,
a conventional procedure in the repertoire for lute and
clavecin—but writing it out in such a way that there is a built-in
ritardando. Charpentier also begins to experiment with textual/
musical repetitions to form shapely, autonomous musical
structures—ariosos and quasi-arias—and even, in two successive
psalms of this group (Psalms 41 and 1), follows his music for the

34

last psalm-verse with reprises of earlier verses, thus creating quasi-*rondeau* designs. By now, too, he has mastered a satisfactory formula—anticipated by Jean Veillot in the motet *Sacris solemniis*—for introducing a work with an instrumental prelude that anticipates the vocal entries to follow, as is exemplified in Example 8.[13] He has also begun to experiment with the treatment of the doxology, often building a *rondeau* out of it by returning several times to the music of the initial 'Gloria Patri' in the course of the later verses. (Later, in such works as the big *Laudate Dominum omnes gentes octo vocibus* of the mid-1690s, he was even to introduce reprises of the initial *psalm* verse's music into the doxology, rounding off the entire composition, not just the Doxology, even more emphatically.)

Ex. 8. *Domine non secundum pour une basse-taille avec 2 violons*
(Cat. 433), bars 1–5, 24–30 (xxvi. 51–51ᵛ)

From the mid-1680s dates an impressive group of psalms for double chorus with double orchestra (Cat. 189–91)—these, like the earlier *petit-chœur* psalms, apparently composed for the

<hr />

[13] Such preludes are discussed at some length in H. W. Hitchcock, 'The Instrumental Music of Marc-Antoine Charpentier,' *Musical Quarterly*, 47 (1961), 58–72, which also includes (as Ex. 1) a complete transcription of the prelude partially reproduced here as Example 8.

Dauphin's chapel. After the death of Queen Marie-Thérèse (30 July 1683), Charpentier composed at least three works in her memory, two motets (Cat. 331 and 409) and—as a companion piece to the latter—a huge *De profundis*. In the 'official' style of the *grand motet* and more than five hundred bars long, it is scored for nine soloists, SATB/SATB double chorus, recorders, strings, and continuo group. The strings are written not in Charpentier's usual four-part texture but for the five parts of the *vingt-quatre violons du roi—dessus, haute-contres, tailles, quintes*, and *basses de violon*—which the Dauphin may in fact have borrowed on the occasion of a memorial service for his mother. Charpentier's airy style of *récit* (a term long used in France, perhaps first in the *ballets de cour*, to signify 'vocal solo', and not implying recitative), more lyrical than that of either Lully or Lalande, is everywhere apparent, as is his emphasis, conforming to French taste, of solos for *basse chantante*. Characteristic is one such solo, accompanied with two obbligato recorders and continuo, at the verse *A custodia matutina usque ad noctem speret Israel in Domino* ('Israel hopes for [the coming of] the Lord as a watchman does for the morning') (Ex. 9).

Even more grand is the contemporaneous *Psalmus 109ᵐᵘˢ: Dixit Dominus 8 vocibus et totidem instrumentis* for eight soloists, SATB/SATB double chorus, and double orchestra of recorders, flutes, and strings, with a continuo group of *basses de violon* and bassoon as well as organ. The celebrated operatic bass soloist Jean Dun is named in the score, and the orchestra is scored à 4; thus this Vespers psalm was probably composed for the Jesuits, as was perhaps the similarly scaled *Psalmus 147* ('Lauda Jerusalem') in Charpentier's next manuscript gathering. The plan of each of these works—like that of virtually all Charpentier's later psalm settings for large forces—resembles that of a *grand motet*, with a careful succession of contrasting *grand-chœur* and *petit-chœur* movements. That of the *Dixit Dominus 8 vocibus* is shown in Table 3.

Most of Charpentier's larger psalm settings of the 1680s and 1690s seem to have been composed for the Jesuits of Saint-Louis, but he also wrote two major motet-psalms in the 1680s for the musicians of Mlle de Guise—*Psalmus David 50ᵐᵘˢ* (later revised for Saint-Louis and retitled *Miserere des Jésuites*) and *Bonum est confiteri Domino/Psalmus David 91ᵘˢ*. These are not only unusually long works—each more than seven hundred

Ex. 9. *De profundis* (Cat. 189), bars 348–63 (xx. 57)

bars—but are exceptional in being scored for six-part chorus, and with consummate mastery. The choral writing alternates between powerful declamatory, homorhythmic texture (but with dynamic inner-part interaction) and imitative counterpoint of great linear integrity. The writing for soloists is equally masterly,

TABLE 3. *The design of the* Dixit Dominus 8 vocibus

Section	Scoring	Bars
1. Prelude	*Tous* [double orch.]	38
2. Dixit Dominus	ATB trio; 2 vns./2 fls. pairs, b.c.	29
3. Virgam virtutis	*Tous*, then orch'l ritornello	43
4. Tecum principium	SSA & ATB trios; 2 vns., b.c.	94
5. Dominis a dextris tuis	*Tous* with orch'l ritornellos	70
6. De torrente in via	AT & BB duos; 2 fls., b.c.	43
7. Simph[onia]	*Tous* [double orch.]	17
8. Gloria Patri	*Tous* with B solos	95
		429

with long, leisurely phrases unrolling in extraordinary arcs of graceful melody, as in one soprano duet of the Psalm 91 setting, at the verse 'Justus ut palma florebit', which opens with the exuberant phrase shown in Example 10.

These two works reveal Charpentier at the height of his powers, and his later psalm settings, by and large, maintain the

Ex. 10. *Bonum est confiteri Domino/Psalmus David* 91[us] (Cat. 195), bars 408–23 (xxii. 64)

The righteous shall flourish like the palm tree.

same level of compositional skill and inspiration. Indeed, some new subtleties appear, especially in text–music relationships—such as a 'tremblant' organ stop to underscore the wicked man gnashing his teeth ('dentibus suis fremet') in a setting of Psalm 111 ('Beatus vir qui timet Dominum') (Cat. 199) and, in a later setting of the same text passage (in Cat. 208), string tremolos reminiscent of the chorus that shivers in 'the iciest spot in Scythia' in Act IV of Lully's *Isis*. There are further nuances of articulation and dynamics, greater fluidity and precision of rhythmic declamation, and firmer tonal harmonies and broader spans of modulation. The mature Charpentier found unique ways of combining a thoroughly profound—and very French—respect for perfect declamation with a lyrical, cantabile—and very Italianate—melodic line; typical is one solo (with muted string accompaniment) for the bass 'Mr Dun' in a Vespers Psalm 110 (*Confitebor à 4 voix et instruments*). In the portion given as Example 11, to the text 'Holy and awesome is his name', note the sensitive contrast between the settings of 'Sanctum' and 'et terrible', and the seemingly inevitable, foreordained closure of the phrase, on to the tonic Bb, at 'nomen ejus'—over which the strings proceed seamlessly to their own cadence, thus forming an effortless but effective punctuation before the appearance of the next half-phrase of text.

Ex. 11. *Confitebor à 4 voix et instruments* (Cat. 225), bars 214–32 (xxvi. 57^v)

Here we might revert to our earlier theme of diversity in Charpentier's music. Among the very latest of Charpentier's psalms are, on the one hand, a pair of Vespers psalms for the convent of Port-Royal—a *Dixit Dominus* and a *Laudate Dominum omnes gentes*—that are of a delectable intimacy; on the other hand, for the Sainte-Chapelle he composed three massive motet-psalms for Matins of Holy Week in 1699 (Cat. 228–30). The Port-Royal pieces are composed for nuns—a trio of soloists (the manuscript names 'Mère de Ste Agathe', 'Melle du Fresnoy', and 'Mère de St Bernard') and a tiny two-part chorus, with organ—and are of a cameo-like delicacy (and, in the *Dixit Dominus*, a charmingly archaic sonority, for it is written in the old-fashioned quasi-parlando *fauxbourdon* style). The Sainte-Chapelle psalms, by contrast, are in Charpentier's most impressively pompous, 'regal' style of massed voices, plus six to nine soloists, full string orchestra, and continuo group.

III

MUSIC FOR THE CHURCH II:
THE MOTETS AND
INSTRUMENTAL WORKS

La pratique en apprend plus que toutes les règles.

Charpentier, *Règles de composition*

IN this chapter I shall consider the music for the church by Charpentier not discussed in Chapter 2; this consists of more than two hundred motets, as well as some instrumental compositions—again, as in that chapter, a daunting number of works to deal with, in a brief book, in any but the most summary and selective way.

Motets

As mentioned in the previous chapter, motets in Charpentier's time were (as they had been for more than two centuries) para-liturgical musical interpolations in the Roman Catholic liturgy. They did not constitute a stylistic genre, the only thing common to them all being the Latin language of their texts. They could be short or long, cast in one movement or several, scored for a few voices or many, with or without obbligato instruments (or orchestra) in addition to the continuo bass. To any given service, motets might be added or not, depending on the solemnity of the occasion and the time or day of the church year, which also determined their texts. These could be general or specific in subject-matter, and derived from a variety of sources, not all of them liturgical or scriptural: composers most often pillaged (or paraphrased) passages from psalms, the Song of Songs, Old and New Testament tales, the lives of saints, and other ecclesiastical writings; they also ransacked the ardent, often perfervid devotional poetry and prose sparked by the Counter-Reformation; not infrequently, they wrote new texts of their own, or were asked to set those of others. Thus the motets of any single composer of the period—especially one as prolific as Charpentier—are apt to be a very mixed bag.

Charpentier's two hundred-odd motets are, indeed, of the greatest imaginable diversity. Here it will be convenient to discuss them in three groups: (1) elevation and 'Domine salvum' motets—specific, it will be recalled, to two moments during the Mass ceremony; (2) 'occasional' motets—for particular occasions in the church year, for individual saints or other persons, or for special events—sacred, pseudo-sacred, or secular; and (3) dramatic motets, which have often been called—not quite accurately—'oratorios'.

Elevation and 'Domine salvum' Motets

The elevation motets—sung during Mass 'à l'heure qu'on lève l'hostie', as Charpentier comments in the margin of his manuscript for an *Elévation à 3 dessus*—and the 'Domine salvum' motets sung at the very end of the Mass—'après la Postcommunion', he says in the manuscripts of two (Cat. 285 and 299)—need not occupy us for long. As explained earlier, these were conventional components of the King's Mass and as such were emulated elsewhere in the realm; although composers applied themselves carefully to elevation motets, in keeping with the solemnity of their eucharistic connection, they also tended to keep them brief, in keeping with their being only a punctuating highlight in the middle of the Sanctus/Benedictus. They tended to set the 'Domine salvum' text—a single psalm verse—even more briefly and often perfunctorily, especially if they were writing for churches or chapels outside the court circle.

Charpentier's forty-eight elevation motets have a wide variety of eucharistic texts but are relatively alike in scoring and scope. Almost all are *petits motets* for few voices, most often a trio (predominantly SSB or ATB), with simple continuo accompaniment, plus occasionally two violins or recorders; thirty of the forty-eight are less than eighty bars long. In other musical respects, however, these elevation motets are rather special—in much the same way, and for the same reason, that Frescobaldi's elevation toccatas differ from his other ones. They reflect the new Counter-Reformational—one might say Jesuitical—emphasis on the Mass as a magical and dramatic 'action', with a transcendent, mystical climax at the consecration of the host and the moment of its transubstantiation. Thus, most of Charpentier's elevations are delicate, hushed, gentle; they address with awe and wonderment the 'true Body' ('Ave verum Corpus'), the 'sacred banquet' ('O sacrum convivium'), the 'angelic bread' ('Panis angelicus'), the 'most merciful Lord Jesus' ('O clementissime Domine Jesu'), the 'most beloved Christ, our sweet Saviour' ('O amantissime salvator noster Jesu dulcis'). Among them are some of Charpentier's most exquisite miniatures, notably a sixty-four-bar 'O pretiosum, o salutiferum, o admirabile convivium' for soprano with two violins and continuo, a sixty-five-bar 'O vere, o bone, o care Jesu' for *haute-contre* and continuo, and—twice as long—an 'O amor, o bonitas, o charitas') for SSB or ATB trio and continuo (Charpentier terming the bass specifically 'une basse chantante'). A few elevations are unusual in being composed for especially large forces, such as one 'Pie Jesu' which is scored for soloists, double choir, and continuo—but this was conceived as part of the big *Messe pour les trépassés*—or the *Elévation à 5 sans dessus de violon*, which is also of exceptional length (312 bars) and contrapuntal ingenuity.

If Charpentier's elevation motets are diverse in texts but similar to each other in tone and scope, the twenty-five 'Domine salvum' motets are the opposite: although by definition all set the same text, they are very diverse in their music. They range from the simplest and briefest *petits motets*—Cat. 304, for two solo voices and continuo, has but twenty bars—to very impressive and comparatively grand ones, particularly those composed as units of Mass settings, such as the *Messe à 8 voix et 8 violons et flûtes*, the *Messe à 4 voix, 4 violins, 2 flûtes, et 2 hautbois, pour Mr Mauroy*, and the *Assumpta est Maria* Mass. Although none is a major masterpiece, as a group they show very well Charpentier's gift for melodic invention: he finds, for instance, any number of different ways—all respectful of the textual rhythm—of setting the opening phrase, as can be suggested by the excerpts in Example 12.

Ex. 12. 'Domine salvum fac regem' themes: (*a*) *Domine salvum* (Cat. 281), bars 1–4 (*dessus* only) (xiv. 45);

(*c*) *Autre Domine* (Cat. 294), bars 1–6
(*dessus* and *bas-dessus* only) (vi. 53ᵛ);

(*d*) *Domine salvum à 3 voix pareilles* (Cat. 302), bars 1–6
(*haute-contre* only) (xxiv. 45)

(*e*) *Domine salvum* (Cat. 303), bars 1–3 (*dessus* only) (xxvii. 14ᵛ)

Occasional Motets

The 'occasions' of Charpentier's eighty-five occasional motets
are many, and of different kinds. About half are specific saints'
days or Church feasts (Easter, All Souls' Day, Christmas,
Purification, Circumcision, Virgin not a Martyr, Confessor not
Pontiff, and the like). A few are special kinds of services such as
catechism or *reposoir* ceremonies.[1] One or another of the feasts of
the Virgin are served by more than a dozen motets addressed to
her. A few motets treat the Trinity (or Christ or the Holy Spirit
alone); three are for Mary Magdalene, one for 'several martyrs'
(*Pour plusieurs martyrs*). Some motets are seasonal, composed for
Lent (*Méditations pour le Carême*) or Eastertide (*Chant joyeux du*

---

[1] Regarding the latter, see, later in this chapter, the discussion of Charpentier's
instrumental religious works.

temps de Pâques; one puzzling group of four—puzzling because the ecclesiastical connotations are unclear—is titled *Quatuor Anni Tempestates* ('The Four Seasons of the Year'). Overtly secular themes are occasionally elaborated (in the name of the Lord, of course). One motet implores the deity for the support of France in battle (*Motet pendant la guerre*); others celebrate royal personages or bemoan their deaths. The recovery of the Dauphin from illness and, a few years later, the King from a dreadful anal fistula evoked from Charpentier motets of gratitude (*Gratiarum actiones ex sacris codicibus excerptae pro restituta serenissimi Galliarum Delphini salute* and *Gratiarum actiones pro restituta Regis christianissimi sanitate an[no] 1686*), the death of the Queen in 1683 one of lamentation (*Luctus de morte augustissimae Mariae Theresiae reginae Galliae*).

It must be admitted that many of the occasional motets—brief, calling for slender forces, setting texts without any particular distinction (or pedigree; the sources of many are unlocated)—are rather prosaic, journeyman compositions, the products of a working composer earning his daily bread with, literally, serviceable compositions. Here, I shall point to those motets that seem to have special interest.

Charpentier's gifts as a melodist are apparent in several slight motets. *Pour plusieurs martyrs* is unique among this group (and very unusual in Charpentier's whole œuvre) in being, as the manuscript's subtitle has it, a 'motet à voix seule sans accompagnement'; it is also noteworthy for the skill with which the composer varies the phrase-lengths, elides the cadences, and shifts the metres in it—all techniques that help keep interesting this work in an extremely restricted medium. Also unusual is a brief 'Gloria in excelsis Deo' for soprano and continuo titled *Pour le catéchisme*, not only for its use of 6/8 metre—seldom found in Charpentier's music—but for the jagged curve of its fanfare-like theme.

Mary Magdalene had a kind of morbid, almost prurient fascination for the seventeenth century. (Think of the many Baroque paintings in which her bare breasts are almost—*almost*—visible under her long hair.) This fascination is reflected in a number of especially poignant, not to say voluptuous, works by Charpentier in which she figures, three of them occasional motets on variant versions of the same text, *Sola vivebat in antris Magdalena lugens* ("The Magdalene, mourning,

46

was living alone in caves'). Of these the first, *Magdalena lugens voce sola cum symphonia*, seems to have pleased both the composer—'bon à exécuter', he wrote on the manuscript—and Brossard, who either made a copy of it himself or had one made. The tonic key is E minor, which for Charpentier had an 'effemmé [*sic*], amoureux et plaintif' quality. (The other Magdalene motets are in A minor—'tendre et plaintif'—and C minor—'obscur et triste'.) *Magdalena lugens* . . . is exceptionally Italianate—not only superficially (with its Italian tempo marking 'adagio', twice) but profoundly, in details of melody, harmony, and intense affective expression. (Prominent in it is that Italian chaconne-bass 'emblem of lament', the descending tetrachord in minor mode.)[2] Its form, too, is especially Italianate, being that of an Italian solo cantata of the mid- to late seventeenth century—like those by Carissimi or even the later Stradella or Alessandro Scarlatti—with a sectional structure in which declamatory recitatives alternate with lyric arias. Its outline is shown in Table 4 (the movement numbers and headings not original).

TABLE 4. *The design of* Magdalena lugens

Section	Text	Metre	Bars
1. Prelude (instruments)		¢	10
2. Recitative 1	Sola vivebat	¢	12
3. Aria 1	O amor meus	¢$\frac{3}{2}$	60
4. Recitative 2	Quis mihi det	¢	17
5. Aria 1 (varied reprise)	Quid retribuam	¢$\frac{3}{2}$	30
6. Aria 2, strophe 1	Magdalena luge	2	25
strophe 2	Plora luge	2	24
7. Recitative 3	Heu, heu!	¢	8
8. Aria 1 (*da capo*)	O amor meus	¢$\frac{3}{2}$	60
			246

In this work, the singer must shift roles between narrator and 'character', exactly as the singer of an Italian cantata must. The opening recitative is scene-setting narration, but in Aria 1 it is the Magdalene herself who speaks. Her yearning lament for the lost Lord—'O my love and my heart's delight'—is expressed by

---

[2] The characterization is that of Ellen Rosand; see her article 'The Descending Tetrachord: An Emblem of Lament', *Musical Quarterly*, 65 (1979), 346–59.

Charpentier in a thoroughly Italianate, liquidly *bel-canto*-style melody, intensified at times by gasping off-beat exclamations (Ex. 13).[3]

Ex. 13. *Magdalena lugens . . .* (Cat. 343), bars 23–38 (viii. 4ᵛ)

[3] Yet another Magdalene motet—equally Italianate, equally sensual—is *Dialogus inter Magdalenam et Jesum*, to be discussed below among the dramatic motets.

48

It should not surprise us to find that the majority of the occasional motets are *petits motets* for one or the other of Charpentier's favourite vocal trios, SSA and ATB. Among these, a few stand out. A *Motet de la Vierge pour toutes ses fêtes*, with a text adapted from the sensuous Song of Songs ('Quam pulchra es, amica mea'), was composed for three nuns (SSA), who are given music of ardent lyricism which bubbles up in a froth of melismata at the final exhortation, *Veni de Libano, columba mea: coronaberis*! ('Come from Lebanon, my dove: you shall be crowned!'). The ten *Méditations pour le Carême*, a unique cycle of Lenten motets for ATB male trio, are a kind of musical *Via Dolorosa* (Stations of the Cross): almost every one of the tiny works (their average length is about sixty bars) is a vignette limning a moment on the tragic path to the Crucifixion and Entombment. Consider this sequence: The scene, one of desolation, is set (1ère Méditation: 'Desolatione desolata est terra') and in it is placed the frail believer (2de: 'Sicut pullus hirundinis sic clamabo'); in the garden of Gethsemane, Christ announces to his disciples his imminent death (3ème: 'Tristis est anima mea'); Judas betrays Christ (4ème: 'Ecce Judas'). The progression is broken by the 5ème Méditation, which takes us back to the Mount of Olives and Peter's denial of Christ ('Cum caenasset Jesus'). Then the sequence resumes: Pilate is persuaded to condemn Christ (6ème Méditation: 'Quaerebat Pilatus dimittere Jesum'); Christ dies on the Cross (7ème: 'Tenebrae factae sunt'); Mary grieves at the foot of the Cross (8ème: 'Stabat mater dolorosa'); Mary Magdalene meets Christ at the tomb (9ème: 'Sola vivebat in antris Magdalena lugens', a setting of a textual variant of *Magdalena lugens . . .*). The cycle is closed with a mini-drama on the tale of Abraham's near-sacrifice of Isaac—surely to be interpreted as an Old Testament type of Christ's own sacrifice. The harmonic language of these *Méditations* is often audaciously Italianate, but the sensitive, predominantly syllabic text settings betray a basically French aesthetic.

The motet celebrating the return to good health of the Dauphin (*Gratiarum actiones ex sacris codicibus excerptae . . .*) is another trio, written for the Dauphin's chapel. (The manuscript mentions the Pièche sisters and the bass Antoine Frison.) Quite long, but also quite stolid and stiff (an uninspired piece of *Gebrauchsmusik*?), it has an instrumentation unusual in

Charpentier's scores: two treble recorders, bass recorder, and a continuo group made up of bass viol, bass violin (probably that peculiarly French bass tuned like a cello but a whole-tone lower, but perhaps the smaller five-string instrument), and 'clavecim'—as Charpentier's manuscript puts it, in a half-Italian/half-French slip of the pen conflating *clavicembalo* and *clavecin*.

A few of the larger occasional motets deserve mention. *In honorem Sancti Ludovici regis Galliae canticum*, dating from the early 1690s, is of exceptional pomp, circumstance, and clamour—as befits a work celebrating Louis IX, crusader king of France from 1226 to 1270, renowned for piety and charity and revered for presiding over the construction of the Sainte-Chapelle (as a reliquary for Christ's crown of thorns, brought from Constantinople during his reign). This is a very grand *grand motet* indeed: it opens with an exceptionally powerful prelude (and, in A B A form, an atypically shaped one); it is more than six hundred bars long and is scored for multiple soloists, large chorus, and elaborate orchestra of winds, strings, and organ; it is resplendent with clarion instrumental fanfares, stentorian vocal-solo virtuosity, energetic choral polyphony, and general musical braggadocio.

Almost as impressive, and with similar expressive content, is another motet in praise of an historic figure—*In honorem Sancti Xaverij canticum*. Dating from the late 1680s, it was certainly composed for the Jesuits, who had a special reverence for St Francis Xavier, one of St Ignatius Loyola's most important collaborators in founding the Society of Jesus. The extravagance with which the saint's virtues are celebrated can be suggested by the fantastic virtuosity demanded of a soprano soloist to open the work (after a *Praeludium*); the text is 'I saw an angel flying amidst the heavens' (Ex. 14).

One of the latest works by Charpentier that is extant (dating from 1698 or 1699) is an immense motet—almost eight hundred bars long, and scored for eight soloists, SATB chorus, recorders, double-reeds, strings, and organ—originally titled *Motet pour l'offertoire de la Messe Rouge*. Thus it was composed for the ceremonial Mass at the opening of the French *Parlement*, celebrated annually in the Sainte-Chapelle and named after the scarlet robes of state worn by the members of the assembly. The original title, however, soon gave way to a less specific one,

Ex. 14. *In honorem Sancti Xaverij canticum* (Cat. 355), bars 23–33 (ix. 44)

Charpentier pasting a slip of paper over the original and, for reasons that remain unclear, retitling the work *Motet pour une longue offrande*. Perhaps the motet had been rejected by the authorities, or perhaps Charpentier wished to disguise its original, occasional destination. But the text is a dead giveaway: clearly topical, it puffs, by association with God the Judge Omnipotent, the purely judicial role to which the *Parlement* had been reduced: 'Paravit Dominus in judicio thronum suum . . . Deus justus et patiens. . . . Justus es, Domine. . . . Justitia et pax osculati sunt [*sic!*] . . .'

Not as grand or as lengthy as these motets but nevertheless requiring five soloists, five-part chorus, two flutes (not recorders but *flûtes allemandes*), and continuo is a finely wrought, quasi-dramatic vignette composed for a Corpus Christ street-altar (*reposoir*) ceremony: 'Oculi omnium sperant in te Domine' (*Pour le S' Sacrement au reposoir*). The characters in this little scene are not named but are clearly identifiable. Hungry supplicants (STB trio) call upon the Lord for help. He responds (B solo), inviting them to the heavenly table. The company of the blessed (*tous*, SSATB) sings ecstatically of celestial happiness. The supplicants (now five, SSATB soloists) look on wistfully, then join the ranks of the blessed (*tous*): 'O nos felices! O nos beati!'

Dramatic Motets

'Oculi omnium . . .' comes close to qualifying among the group of Charpentier's compositions that I call 'dramatic motets': it is obviously a moralistic drama. But it remains an abstract one, in which the listener must infer the characters in the drama. The dramatic motets proper have characters who are concretely, specifically identified, and the works are actually shaped as dramas—with dialogue, implicit action, and one or more narrators (*historici*) to link the 'scenes' since, though dramas, these motets are unstaged—though in some the 'drama' consists only in dialogue between named characters or groups. These works have generally been termed 'oratorios', by analogy with the similar compositions of Charpentier's mentor Carissimi which were clearly the models for some of the Parisian's. But Charpentier's were not written for oratory meetings (as were Carissimi's), but, rather, for use in church services as motets (as is made explicitly clear in marginalia in the manuscripts of many); nor are all of them 'sacred stories'—dramatic canvases unrolling in time and peopled with characters involved in actions and events—so the term commonly used by the French for them, *histoires sacrées*, is an indefensible overgeneralization. Charpentier himself used, besides *motet*, such terms as *historia*, *canticum*, and *dialogus*—the first of these implying a lengthy, dramatic work, the second (translatable more accurately as 'song' than 'canticle') a similar but slighter, or, in some instances, a more reflective and less dramatic work, and the last a simply structured discussion—a dialogue—between individuals or groups. Diversity reigns in this class of composition as in others by Charpentier: apart from their dramatic orientation, his thirty-five dramatic motets are immensely varied—in subject, in length, in style, and in performance forces.

Closest to Carissimi's models are a group of early *historiae* based on the biblical tales of Judith and Holofernes (*Judith sive Bethulia liberata*), Esther and Ahasuerus (*Historia Esther*), the Prodigal Son (*Filius prodigus*), the Last Judgement (*Extremum Dei judicium*), Abraham and Isaac (*Sacrificium Abrahae*), the deaths of Saul and Jonathan (*Mors Saülis et Jonathae*), and Joshua's conquest of the Promised Land (*Josue*). The brief *Dialogus inter Magdalenam et Jesum*, possibly a fragment from a larger work (its sole source is a copyist's manuscript), also belongs to this group: it has the same Italianate atmosphere and almost steamy sensuality as *Magdalena lugens . . .*, with the Magdalene sobbing in grief ('Hei mihi, infelix Magdalena') and Christ remonstrating—but gently and lyrically—'Noli me tangere!'

Though the debts to Carissimi are many in this group of motets, Charpentier goes beyond his Roman master in instrumental requirements (such as the trumpets that sound the Day of Judgement in *Extremum Dei judicium* or the double orchestra of the prelude to *Josue*); in closed formal designs (especially A B A and larger *rondeau*-like patterns); and especially in harmonic audacity: nowhere in Carissimi's oratorios do we hear wrenching augmented sixths or octaves (asterisked in Ex. 15) of the sort with which the chorus greets the news of Saul's and Jonathan's deaths. (The excerpt can also suggest the frequent rhymed Latin in which Charpentier's unknown 'librettists' recast the prose of the Vulgate.)

Two non-biblical motets also belong to this group of early

53

(O unhappy and harsh fate!
O cruel and bitter death!)

works that are primarily Italianate in style. One is the splendid *Caecilia virgo et martyr octo vocibus*—the largest of four dramatic motets Charpentier composed around the apocryphal (if ancient) account of the conversion to Christianity, by the second- or third-century Roman virgin Cecilia, of her husband Valerianus and his brother Tiburtius, and their subsequent martyrdom.[4] (In this motet, her role as patron saint of music is played up, as it were, by an especially rich orchestration of the final chorus of praise for her, which includes—at the mention of an organ—a brief written-out organ part, most unusual in Charpentier's works.) The other is *Pestis Mediolanensis* ('The Plague of Milan'). This begins with a description of the horrors of the plague that ravaged Milan in 1576–7, then turns to the selfless

---

[4] The others are *In honorem Caeciliae, Valeriani et Tiburtij canticum* (Cat. 394) and two titled *Caecilia virgo et martyr* (Cat. 413, 415).

heroism, during it, of St Charles Borromeo, archbishop of Milan at the time. Like many others of Charpentier's dramatic motets (and the Italian oratorios in their background), *Pestis Mediolanensis* is in two balanced and contrasting parts. Part I is a gruesome portrayal of the plague-ridden city, couched in some of the most intensely affective and startling chromatic music to be found in Charpentier's scores. Part II is an almost ecstatic choral exhortation to praise St Charles on his feast day, for which—and possibly in centenary commemoration of his charity during the plague—the work was probably composed.

Besides the *petit motet* he composed on the death of the Queen of France (*Luctus de morte . . .*), Charpentier also wrote a giant *grand motet* of the dramatic type: *In obitum augustissimae necnon piissimae Gallorum reginae lamentum*. Its manuscript is followed immediately by that for the very lengthy *De profundis* scored for similarly large forces and in similar Lullian fashion; the two works were probably performed, one after the other, by the Dauphin's chapel musicians in a memorial service. In the 'Lament' the drama is allegorical, for the principal characters are Faith, Hope, and Charity (an SSS trio), besides an Angel, a Narrator, and another trio (ATB), 'Three Members of the Populace'. The orchestral and choral writing is undeniably French; however, the solos—especially the recitatives—and the trios, as well as the two-part structure of the work, derive from the Italian oratorio tradition.

A number of the dramatic motets of the 1680s and 1690s are *petits motets*—most often vocal trios, usually with two violins or recorders as well as continuo. For whatever reason, the subjects are mostly drawn from the New Testament. Thus we find an *In resurrectione Domini Nostri Jesu Christi*, with Mary Magdalene, the Other Mary, and the Angel at the tomb; an *In circumcisione Domini*, subtitled 'Dialogus inter angelum et pastores'; two other dialogues in which Christ is the principal figure, along with a Hungry Man and a Thirsty Man (*Dialogus inter esurientem, sitientem et Christum* and an *Élévation* ('Famem meam quis replebit?')); and the like.

In the mid-1680s Charpentier turned back to a Christmastide text he had set as a *petit motet* early in his career; it begins with the lovely line 'Frigidae noctis umbra totum orbem tegebat' ('The dark of the icy night covered all the earth'). On this text he wrote new music for Mlle de Guise, to produce *In nativitatem*

Domini Nostri Jesu Christi canticum, one of his most attractive works in any genre. The 'Interlocutores', his score tells us, are an Angel, Shepherds, and a Narrator. After a brief prelude for two violins or flutes and continuo, the Narrator—represented by two sopranos (such multi-voice narration not being uncommon in these works)—describes in recitative how, on the bitter-cold night when Christ is born, an angel appears to the shepherds of Judea, who are terrified. The Angel (S solo) reassures them, in a lilting air with instrumental ritornellos, and urges them to go to Bethlehem to see for themselves. The Shepherds (small chorus à 5) react excitedly—'Surgamus! festinemus! eamus usque Bethleem!'—and set off, their journey being symbolized, with mock naïveté, by a little march for the instruments. Having arrived (so a Br. solo narrator tells us), they fall on their knees in awe and offer to the Christ Child a 'crude but devout song'—a strophic air straight out of the French *noël* tradition (Ex. 16), each of its strophes repeated by the chorus (such a polyphonic repetition of a solo stanza itself deriving from the French chanson/air tradition). A postlude for the instruments concludes the motet.

TABLE 5. *The design of* In nativitatem Domini Nostri Jesu Christi canticum

Section	Scoring	Elements of style
1. Prelude	(instruments)	3 metre; A B A form
2. Recitative (Narrator)	SS duo; b.c.	simple recitative
3. Air (Angel)	S solo; 2 vns., b.c.	quasi-*rondeau* form
4. Chorus (Shepherds)	Chorus à 6; 2 vns., b.c.	contrapuntal; quasi-*rondeau* form
5. March	(instruments)	¢ metre; A b A c A form
6. Recitative (Narrator)	Br. solo; 2 vns., b.c.	arioso
7. Air (Shepherd)	S solo; b.c.	strophic; binary form
8. Chorus (Shepherds)	Chorus à 5; 2 vns., b.c.	homophonic; binary form
9. Postlude	(instruments)	3 metre; free form

There are extremely interesting aspects of form and aesthetic in this work. Its nine sections are outlined in Table 5. Charpentier's aesthetic ideal of diversity obviously underlies this plan: not only is none of the sections preceded or followed by

Ex. 16. *In nativitatem Domini Nostri Jesu Christi canticum* (Cat. 414),
bars 257–80 (vi. 94ᵛ)

(Hail, tiny Lordling!
Hail, tender newborn King!
Now all creation sing
　Thy praise and worth.

Thou heaven dost desert
And in this humble birth
Comest to men on earth
　Our sins to bear)

another in the same style or medium, but each of the apparently
repetitive styles and media (recitative, solo air, chorus, instrumental movement) is stylistically different at each appearance.
Another formal/aesthetic principle is also at work here (as in
many of Charpentier's works): symmetry. This is shown in
Fig. 1.

　The pastoral emphasis in this version of the Christmas story
is characteristic of France in general in the *grand siècle*. (Not
for nothing does M. Jourdain, Molière's oafish *bourgeois*

57

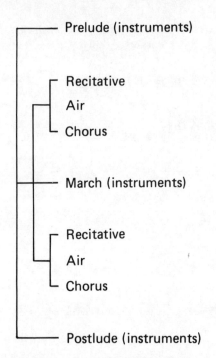

┌─── Prelude (instruments)
│
│   ┌─ Recitative
│   │
├────────┼─ Air
│   │
│   └─ Chorus
│
├─── March (instruments)
│
│   ┌─ Recitative
│   │
├────────┼─ Air
│   │
│   └─ Chorus
│
└─── Postlude (instruments)

FIG. 1. Symmetrical structure of *In nativitatem Domini Nostri Christi canticum*

gentilhomme, react to the entertainment his music master has presented with the complaint, 'Pourquoi toujours des bergers? On ne voit que cela par-tout.') Charpentier reflects this fashion (here and elsewhere). Not only did he turn yet again (in Cat. 421) to the Christmastide text he had already set twice before (Cat. 393 and 414); in two other, larger Christmas motets he again emphasized the Judean shepherds: *In nativitatem Domini canticum* and *Dialogus inter angelos et pastores Judeae in nativitatem Domini*. Both are for substantial forces—soloists, chorus, orchestra of recorders and strings—and both have evocative, programmatic instrumental movements depicting the night Christ was born and, the next morning, the shepherds' awakening ('Réveil des bergers'); the *symphonie* 'Nuit' in the first of these motets is an inspired representation of nocturnal stillness, with muted-string scoring, murmuring, meandering melodic lines, and somnolent, slow-moving rhythms, rocking gently in slurred pairs of minims (Ex. 17).

This Christmastide motet exemplifies well the bipartite
structure common to many of the dramatic motets. Here, the
two complementary halves of the work are related as Old and
New Testaments: the pleas of the 'Chorus of the Just' for
salvation, the reassurance by the Lord (a bass soloist), and the
apocalyptic, heaven-splitting release of the Deity (chorus and
instruments) in the first half are precisely counterbalanced, in
the second, by the fear and wonderment of the Judean
shepherds ('Chorus Pastorum'), the reassurance by the Angel

59

(an *haute-contre* soloist), and the ultimate transcendent exaltation over the Saviour's birth (chorus and instruments). This bipartite division is musically supported tonally, the sombre predominant C minor mode of the first half shifting to the blazing arc-light of C major in the second.

Let me conclude this discussion of the dramatic motets with a consideration of the two that are the best known—and with good reason, for they are among Charpentier's finest works. One is *Le Reniement de St Pierre* (St Peter's Denial [of Christ]), probably an early work;[5] the other—*Judicium Salomonis* (The Judgment of Solomon)—is a very late one.

Whoever prepared the Latin text of *Le Reniement* drew cunningly on all four of the principal New Testament evangelists to fashion a dramatic account of the threefold denial of Christ by Peter, and of his remorse thereafter. Charpentier responded with a masterly setting, which, however, calls for only modest performance forces—soloists, chorus, and organ—and is decidedly Italianate in style (hence probably early). His characterizations are very sharp, and he seizes every possible opportunity to dramatize and intensify the text with his music. For Jesus's words he writes music of noble dignity, as opposed to that for Peter's peevish protests. He builds the 'denial scene' like an operatic episode; it culminates in a dramatically agitated quartet, with Peter insistently, almost hysterically, denying to his three accusers any connection with Christ. Then the cock crows, and Christ gazes sombrely at Peter (a touch not found in the biblical accounts). To the poignant words embodying Peter's remorse—*flevit amare* ('he wept bitterly')—Charpentier composed a final chorus celebrated for its purity of melodic line, contrapuntal integrity, and harmonic pungency.

Judicium Salomonis was composed in 1702 for the same occasion as the *Motet pour une longue offrande*—the Messe Rouge of the French *Parlement*. Its unknown 'librettist' adapted from I Kings 3 the tale of Solomon's wise judgment when faced with two women, each claiming maternity of a single child; the implication that this be an exemplar for the judicial *Parlement*

---

[5] The unique manuscript, without composer attribution, is a copy once in the possession of Brossard, who perhaps is responsible for the anomalous French title (the motet's text being, of course, in Latin). Brossard attributes the work unequivocally to Charpentier in the entry for it in the catalogue of his music library—later annexed to the royal collection—and describes it accurately as 'une histoire ou un oratorio à l'italienne . . . à 5 voix CCATB cum organo'.

members is made specific near the conclusion of the work when they are addressed directly: *vos autem purpurati* ('likewise, ye empurpled ones'). In two parts, about thirty-five minutes long, and composed for vocal soloists, chorus, woodwinds, strings, and varied *basse continue, Judicium Salomonis* is one of Charpentier's most carefully worked and most impressively realized compositions. The prelude to its 'Seconde Partie'— another piece of 'night music'—is especially striking: representing the night when God appeared to Solomon in a dream, it is scored for gentle recorders and muted strings and is a most evocative nocturne, remarkable especially for the almost mystical richness, unusual even for Charpentier, of the harmonies with which it ends.[6]

Instrumental Religious Works

Apart from overtures and *airs de ballet* for Molière's troupe, Charpentier had little reason to compose independent instrumental music. Never attached directly to the royal court, he had no opportunity to write *symphonies* or ballet music for the *vingt-quatre violons*. Not an instrumentalist but a singer, he had no occasion to compose *pièces de viole* or *de clavecin* to demonstrate his virtuosity in the *concerts du dimanche*. Nevertheless, he did leave a body of works, both sacred and secular, for instrumental ensembles, among them some of exceptional interest and beauty.

About twenty independent sacred instrumental compositions merit our attention here (leaving aside the very large number of preludes and programmatic *symphonies* in sacred vocal works). Before turning to these as such, however, let me summarize aspects of Charpentier's instrumentation and orchestration. His autographs are a treasure-house of information about these matters, for almost all his scores are exceptionally precise and completely written-out—infinitely more detailed and illuminating than the scores of Lully or Lalande, for example (by whom we have almost no autographs, in any case).

---

[6] This passage is reproduced (as Ex. 9) in Hitchcock, 'The Latin Oratorios', and, of course, in the published edition of the entire work, ed. Hitchcock (New Haven, Connecticut (now Madison, Wisconsin): A-R Editions, 1964).

The instruments Charpentier calls for shquld not surprise us: strings of the violin family, including the treble *dessus*, the viola-range *haute-contre*, *taille*, and *quinte*, and the French *basse de violon* (but no double-bass); viols of similar ranges, including both *basse de viole* and *violone*; recorders of several sizes and (much less often) treble tranverse flute; oboe, bassoon, crumhorn, and serpent (the two last-named cited only once or twice); treble and bass trumpets; timpani, theorbo (specified only twice), harpsichord, and organ. The string group is sometimes to be muted; as we have seen, Charpentier (along with Lully, and perhaps even before him) is one of the first composers to call for such mutes—the *sourdines* for all the strings that characterize several 'night-music' *symphonies*, the accompaniments of a few *récits* in theatrical works, and the setting à 4 of the *noël* 'Or nous dites Marie'.

Charpentier's many *petit-motet*-style compositions often include, along with the continuo (which usually, in such works, is an organ alone), pairs of unspecified treble instruments (in G1 clefs) as obbligato instruments;[7] often, however, these are specified—most often as violins or recorders (or paired violin *and* recorder on each of the two parts), occasionally as viols. Slightly larger works, including a chorus as well as soloists, usually call for a four-part string group, often merely doubling the voice parts but also sometimes fleshing out the sonorities as independent *ripieno* parts, and of course serving independently for preludes, ritornellos, and *symphonies*. The large orchestra Charpentier most often wrote for, however, is one of strings doubled by woodwinds (recorders, oboes, and bassoons); its basic texture is most often an Italianate one of four parts (in G1, C1, C2, and F4 clefs).[8] However, some of the largest sacred works dating from the very late 1670s and into the 1680s,

[7] Clefs are indicated herein by letter (G = G clef, F = F clef, etc.) and number of staff line, reading up (1 = lowest line, 2 = next-lowest line, etc.). G1 = 'French violin' clef: first-line G.

[8] This has led to controversy among editors and scholars of his music: should the two middle string parts be played by violas and only the top part by violins, or should the two top parts be assigned to violins, *à l'italienne*? Only once or twice, in the many thousands of bars of Charpentier's orchestral scores, does the second-highest (*haute-contre*) part dip below the violin's G string (and indeed even the *taille* parts lie rather high in the viola range), yet some French scholars argue for a realization by violin I, violas I and II, and bass violin; see especially Jean Duron, 'L'Orchestre de Marc-Antoine Charpentier', *Revue de musicologie*, 73/3 (1987), 23–65.

apparently composed for the Dauphin, do include the texture à 5 of the court's *vingt-quatre violons*; so does the Lullian tragedy *Médée*. As with Lully, trumpets and drums are elaborative additions to the basic orchestra, reserved generally for ceremonial music 'de triomphe' (to borrow from the title of a *Marche de triomphe*).

As an orchestrator, Charpentier was distinctly a colourist. Although he wrote no concertos as such, the concerto principle of opposed instrumental combinations is the heart of his orchestration technique. Most common is a simple opposition of the orchestral *grand chœur* (*tous*) with a soloistic *petit chœur*, the former in four or five parts, the latter usually in three (two treble parts, one bass). Almost as often, a *grand chœur* of strings and doubling woodwinds is opposed to an unmixed group from one or the other family. In the majestic *pièces d'occasion* or *de triomphe* including trumpets and timpani, we often find contrasts not only between *grand chœur* and *petit chœur* but between them and the combined forces of winds, brasses, strings, and drums—an *encore plus grand chœur*, we might say. A number of compositions for few voices include both violins and viols, Charpentier exploiting quite consciously the differences in their timbres. Finally, a polychoral treatment of two equal orchestras is not uncommon.

Among Charpentier's sacred instrumental works, the most fascinating from the standpoint of instrumentation and orchestration is the *Messe pour plusieurs instruments au lieu des orgues*. An early work, it has all the earmarks of a youthfully self-conscious demonstration of virtuoso control over varied instrumental ensembles. Cast in the unusual form—in fact, it seems to be unique, in French Baroque-era music—of an orchestral Mass (rather than the traditional organ Mass), it consists of *alternatim* versets and independent movements for a rich complement of woodwinds and strings—octave, treble, and bass recorders, transverse flutes, oboes, bass crumhorn, and four-part string orchestra. Regrettably, the unique manuscript source is incomplete. Even so, more than ten different ensembles are called for in the movements that are extant: versets—to alternate with others 'pour les prêtres'—for the Kyrie and Gloria, an 'Offerte à deux chœurs', a possibly incomplete 'Sanctus pour tous les instruments', and the conclusion of another movement, probably an Agnus Dei. Charpentier's manuscript is characteristically specific about details of instrumentation, and in this work, as occasionally elsewhere, his concern for nuances of sonority and balance of timbres leads him even to specify the number of players per part. The Kyrie 4 verset, for instance, is scored for a four-part wind band, the parts to be taken respectively by (1) two treble recorders and one transverse flute (G1), (2) one transverse flute (C1), (3) one transverse flute (C2), and (4) four bass recorders (F4). The unusual weight of the bass part reflects its being a *cantus firmus* part (all in whole notes, moreover) deriving from the Kyrie melody of the plainsong Mass 'Cunctipotens genitor Deus'. The '5ème Kyrie' (*recte* '2ème Christe') is scored 'pour les violons du petit chœur'—the concertino group of soloists, as opposed to the full orchestra—and again the number of players is specified: two first violins (G1), one second violin (G1), and two basses (F4).

Besides the *Messe pour plusieurs instruments . . .*, Charpentier's sacred instrumental works consist of sets of pieces for Corpus Christi street-altar ceremonies and consecrations of bishops, offertories and *alternatim* versets for Masses, antiphons for Office services, an *Ouverture pour l'église*, and two groups of *noël* settings.

Two of the three sets of compositions for Fête-Dieu ceremonies (*Pour un reposoir*, Cat. 508, and *Symphonies pour un reposoir*) include an overture (of the Lullian bipartite type, with a grave duple-time section followed by a quicker, fugal triple-time one), versets of a hymn to alternate with others sung by the clergy, and an allemande (that of the second set no longer surviving). The third set (Cat. 523, also titled *Pour un reposoir*) begins similarly, with an *Ouverture dès que la procession paraît*, followed this time by a motet ('Ave verum Corpus', Cat. 329). Charpentier's marginalia let us imagine the ceremony clearly. A temporary altar on a supporting stand—the *reposoir*—is positioned at some prominent street-corner. Near it is an instrumental ensemble—strings, flutes, harpsichord. Into view comes the procession, a banner at its head (the *Symphonies pour un reposoir* begin with an 'Ouverture dès qu'on voit la bannière'), with priests bearing the Holy Sacrament. 'As soon as the procession appears' (according to the title of the third *reposoir* set), the instruments begin an overture: 'things must be worked out so that the Holy Sacrament is placed [on the altar] before the conclusion of the . . . overture, which then will serve as

64

prelude to the motet [or hymn] that follows'.[9] After the motet or hymn is sung, a benediction is said, and the procession moves on. 'After the benediction, and when the priests are far enough away not to hear them any more, the strings are to play an allemande'.[10]

The tone of these Fête-Dieu pieces is appropriately grave and ceremonious: the allemande that survives is an 'Allemande grave'; the second section of the overture of the third set is to be taken 'lentement'; the instrumental hymn-versets are almost all conservative *cantus-firmus* settings of the traditional plainsong hymn melodies.

Similar in tone are three Lullian overtures *pour le sacre d'un évêque*—'for the consecration of a bishop'. The first of these— for performance while the bishop is robed ('Ouverture pendant qu'il s'habille')—has a companion piece, a trisectional, canzona-like 'Offrande pour un sacre'; both are scored in the five-part court-orchestra manner. The second, which is to be repeated until the bishop goes to the altar ('Recommencez jusqu'à ce que l'évêque aille à l'autel') is also paired with an offertory— *Offertoire pour le sacre d'un évêque à 4 parties de voix et d'instruments*—this one, however, a motet, on a text beginning, appropriately, 'Ecce sacerdos magnus'. The third is a noble work, very French in expressive quality but not in Lullian-overture form; rather, in three broad sections, the first a stately march in C major, the second a lively, danceable one in triple time which explores other keys, with much *grand-chœur* vs. *petit-chœur* competition, and the third a duple-time C major conclusion. Somewhat surprisingly, although the earliest overture of the three (Cat. 518, from the late 1670s) is scored à 5, the two later ones (Cat. 536 and 537, from the early 1690s), are scored for Charpentier's four-part ensemble.

Charpentier's manuscript titles for two of his five extant orchestral antiphons, serving as versets to replace chanted antiphons at Vespers, confirm the Parisian practice, at the time, of placing such antiphons *after* the psalms they accompany: *Après Confitebor [Psalm 110]: antienne* . . . and *Après Beati omnes [Psalm*

[9] 'Ouverture dès que la procession paraît. . . . Il faut faire en sorte que le St Sacrement soit pausé [*sic*] avant que l'ouverture . . . finisse, ce qui servira de prélude au motet suivant' (title and marginalia in Cat. 523).

[10] 'Après la bénédiction et que les prêtres seront assez loin pour ne les plus entendre, les violons joueront une allemande' (marginal note in Cat. 515).

126]: antienne . . . . Four of these pieces are sober, postludial pieces; the one for 'Beati omnes', however, is an unabashed, triple-metre dance movement in binary form; only its fugal beginning lends it a touch of learned seriousness (Ex. 18).

Ex. 18. *Après Beati omnes* . . . (Cat. 517), bars 1–11 (xviii. 28)

An *Offerte pour l'orgue et pour les violons, flûtes et hautbois* is stylistically close to the 'Offerte à deux chœurs' of the *Messe pour plusieurs instruments* . . . (with which early work it is contemporaneous) in its massive block-like opposition of winds and strings, its drone-like basses, and its sectional-canzona design. It also has a feature unique in Charpentier's manuscripts: an almost completely written-out organ part (as opposed to the brief passage in the big Cecilian motet, Cat. 397). This is not as exciting as it sounds: the organ often simply doubles the treble winds (recorders and oboes) as well as the continuo basses (serpents, crumhorn, and bassoon); any independent material it has is comparatively uninteresting.

The manuscripts of two groups of *Noëls sur les instruments* flank the scores of the O-Antiphons, as mentioned earlier, and were written to be performed with them during Christmas week. Both groups are for recorders, four-part strings, and continuo. The first set includes arrangements à 4 of 'O créateur', 'Laissez paître vos bêtes', and 'Vous qui désirez sans fin'; the second, 'Les Bourgeois de Châtre' (two settings, one crossed out as not 'le bon'), 'Où s'en vont ces gais bergers', 'Joseph est bien marié', 'Or nous dites, Marie', 'A la venue de Noël', and 'Une jeune pucelle'. These carols are Charpentier at his most deliciously insouciant, most purely French best.[11]

---

[11] As independent chamber compositions, these add up to an attractive suite and have been so published (*Noëls pour les instruments*, ed. H. W. Hitchcock (Vienna, 1972)).

IV
MUSIC FOR THE CHAMBER

La chanson que je vous envoie . . . a présentement un . . .
grand cours à Paris[;] l'air est du fameux Mr Charpentier,
qui a un si grande connaissance de toutes les beautés de la
musique.

Donneau de Visé (October 1689)

As a composer for the Comédie-Française, the devout Mlle de
Guise, the chapel musicians of the Dauphin, the Jesuits of
Saint-Louis, and the Sainte-Chapelle du Palais, Charpentier
had few opportunities to write chamber music. Nevertheless, we
have from him a small body of secular compositions for the
chamber, both vocal—*airs sérieux et à boire* and cantatas—
and instrumental—miscellaneous ensemble works including a
charming *concert* for viol consort and a magnificent *sonate* for
eight instruments. These chamber works are the subject of the
present chapter.

Vocal Chamber Works

Charpentier's vocal chamber music consists of two groups of
compositions, one rooted in French tradition, the other in
Italian. The first group consists of about thirty of the slight
songs, mostly for solo voice and continuo, that were known
generically in the later years of the seventeenth century as *airs
sérieux et à boire*. The second group consists of eight compositions
—five to Italian texts, two to French, one to Latin—which may
be called 'cantatas', using that term (which Charpentier did not)
to imply nothing more precise than secular vocal chamber music
of Italianate stamp, without suggesting structure or size.

Unlike his work in every other genre, the airs of Charpentier mostly appeared in print. Eleven were tipped into as many issues of the *Mercure galant* between 1678 and 1695; its editor was Donneau de Visé, a man exceptionally sympathetic to Charpentier, probably because of their successful collaborations on works for the Comédie-Française. Other airs by Charpentier were published in song anthologies of the early eighteenth century, especially two periodical series issued by the Ballard firm, *Recueil d'airs sérieux et à boire de différents auteurs* (1695–1704) and *Meslanges de musique latine, françoise et italienne* (1726–9). A few survive in manuscript form (only two in Charpentier's hand).

These airs constitute a virtual compendium of the various types of chamber song popular in Paris in the last quarter of the seventeenth century. Charpentier wrote no *airs de cour*: their heyday—which had been a long one, beginning with Adrian Le Roy's *Livre d'airs de cour* of 1571—had essentially ended with the volume published by Michel Lambert in 1660 (although as late as 1689 Lambert was to publish a final retrospective collection). Charpentier did, however, write about two dozen examples of the *air sérieux*—sometimes called *air tendre*, occasionally just *air* or *récit* (an old term, as noted earlier, for 'vocal solo' in the *ballet de cour*)—which had replaced the *air de cour* as the principal genre of small-scale but somewhat sophisticated French song. He also set a handful of the less-high-flown lyric poems that had diverted Parisians for a century or more—*vaudevilles, chansons à danser, musettes*, and *chansonettes*. And, reflecting a revival in popularity (in Paris, if not at court), from the 1660s on, of bacchic songs, he composed a few *airs à boire*, with texts of rough humour, music of popularesque appeal.

I have called these airs slight, and most of them are; but one is surprised, as in other genres worked by Charpentier, by their range of both textual and musical expression. Some are no more than pleasantly vacuous, but others are truly charming, and a few transcend the conventional limits of their genre in poetic elegance and musical significance.

The texts of Charpentier's *airs sérieux* belong to a tradition of French lyric poetry going all the way back to the troubadours.

Love, occasionally requited but more often not, is the main topic. Shepherds and shepherdesses are the central characters. Their habitats are leafy boscages or verdant meadows, pleasant slopes or rocky gorges. Birds twitter, leaves tremble, brooks burble. Musettes or flutes are always at the ready, or being told to keep silent. Springtime always seems nigh. Birds tune their song to the murmur of the forest streamlet. Nightingales people the pines, warbling away—but perhaps they should flee lest they die of envy at Climène's sweet voice . . . And Sylvie and Tircis are separated by gods jealous of their happiness . . . Nor should assiduous rivals imagine Amaryllis is faithful to any among them: she wants none . . . And I—I am hopelessly in love with the very one who torments me. . . .

The texts of the *airs à boire* are, of course, another matter. Colin, drunk, lifts his sleeping shepherdess's skirt to take his pleasure; she pardons him: one must make excuses for good wine . . . Never mind the skimpy grape harvest, sons of Bacchus: our wine will be so fine, so divine, so potent, so rich, that one glass will equal a pitcherful of any other . . . The sodden old lady has fine little red eyes, a big slack mouth, a pretty retroussé nose . . . And you, comrade Grégoire—do you intend to sleep forever, instead of laughing and drinking and listening to the *glougloux* of the bottle? . . .

Most of the authors seem to have been poetasters, their names not even mentioned in the prints. However, the *Mercure galant* made sure its readers knew that 'l'illustre M^r de La Fontaine' had indited the poem of 'Brillants fleurs naissez' (if also 'Mlle Castille' that of 'Ah! qu'ils sont courts les beaux jours'). And in three successive issues of the monthly (January–March 1681) there appeared, as Donneau de Visé put it, 'une chose fort ancienne, et pourtant toute nouvelle . . . ancienne pour les vers, et très nouvelle pour l'air': a series of three airs by Charpentier on stanzas of *Le Cid*, by the great Pierre Corneille.

The *airs sérieux* are almost all for soprano and continuo, the instrumentation of the latter never being specified.[1] However, the La Fontaine setting and several variants of it (it must have caught on, and invited parodies) are for unaccompanied single voice, as are a *musette* ('Faites trêve à vos chansonettes') and a

---

[1] Over the years, the lute tablature of the accompaniments for *airs de cour* had given way to staff notation (which was retained in the later airs), suggesting perhaps that the harpsichord had become the preferred instrument.

vaudeville ('Qu'il est doux, charmante Climène'). 'Allons sous ce verd feuillage' and 'Tout renaît, tout fleurit' are both for two sopranos and continuo. Of the five *airs à boire*, three are trios— 'Beaux petits yeux d'écarlate', 'Fenchon, la gentille Fenchon', and 'Veux-tu, compère Grégoire'—while 'Ayant bu du vin clairet' is for SB duet with continuo, 'Consolez-vous, chers enfants de Bacchus' for an unaccompanied bass.

The form of almost all the *airs sérieux*, as of a few of the bacchic airs, is a binary structure inherited from the *air de cour*— essentially A B form, but with various permutations of *reprises* (repetitions of one or the other of the two sections), *petites reprises* (repetitions of only the last phrase of a section), and thematic returns (producing a 'rounded binary' form that might be represented as Ax Bx). In contrast to the earlier *airs de cour*, however, the *airs sérieux* generally have but a single stanza, and the elaborately ornamented *doubles* characteristic of the *airs de cour* are not found at all. The vocal line of 'Sans frayeur dans ce bois' is in binary form, with both parts repeated; however, the *Mercure*'s annotator rightly calls the air 'une fort agréable chaconne', for it is laid over a four-bar chaconne bass (to be repeated nineteen times) (Ex. 19*a*) very similar to the one underlying Monteverdi's *Zefiro torna* (Ex. 19*b*). The piquant

Ex. 19*a*. Basse obligée of Charpentier, 'Sans frayeur dans ce bois' (Cat. 467), *Mercure galant* (Mar. 1680), between pp. 288 and 289

Ex. 19*b*. Chaconne bass of Monteverdi, *Zefiro torna* (Madrigal Book IX); metre reduced and pitch transposed up one tone

'Auprès du feu l'on fait l'amour', a tiny, single-stanza *chansonette* printed posthumously in Ballard's *Meslanges de musique . . .* (1728), is unusual in its ‖: A :‖ b A design, and is nicely diversified tonally (considering its minuscule dimensions) with a detour in the middle section—away from (and back to) the tonic—that is handled in an artfully artless way (Ex. 20). (The twenty-eight-bar length of the little song is slightly less than the airs' average.)

Ex. 20. 'Auprès du feu l'on fait l'amour' (Cat. 446), 'Chansonette, de feu Monsieur Charpentier', *Meslanges de musique . . .* (Paris: J.-B.-C. Ballard, 1728), 21

(You can make love as well on the hearth as among the ferns, so don`t wait, lovely shepherdess, until spring returns to choose a good shepherd: you can make love as well on the hearth as among the ferns)

Rondeaux are also found—with a single contrasting *couplet* (A b A) as in 'Ah! qu'ils sont courts les beaux jours', 'Oiseaux de ces bocages', and 'Rendez-moi mes plaisirs', or with two (A b A c A) as in 'Allons sous ce verd feuillage'. In both 'Oiseaux de ces bocages' and 'Rendez-moi mes plaisirs' the *rondeau* proper (the A section) and the *couplet* (b) are stylistically differentiated, one being in recitative, the other in a more lyric, airy style. This is also true of the very fine, passionate 'Tristes déserts, sombre retraite', which brings to mind—in its ornamentation (more generous than usual) and its high incidence of yearning *ports de voix*—the finest *airs de cour* of Lambert. On the other hand, in the exceptionally long 'Non, non, je ne l'aime plus', even more Italianate recitative and 'air' styles alternate several times, and in fact the work resembles in design and dimensions an Italian solo cantata, its 143 bars divided thus:

A	b	A	c	d	e	A′
(air)	(rec.)	(air)	(rec.)	(air)	(rec.)	(air)

(But the double recurrence of A is as much a French *rondeau* technique as one of an Italian rondo aria.) Even closer in some ways to an Italian manner is 'Ruisseau qui nourris dans ce bois', with a 'brook' of a continuo-bass line purling in continuous quavers from start to finish, and a wave-like melodic line which flowers twice into melismata on the very word 'onde'. (But its otherwise wholly syllabic setting of the text is distinctly French.)

Unique among the *airs sérieux* are the three *Airs sur des stances du Cid*.[2] In both text and music, they form a coherent set, to be performed together. The texts are successive stanzas (Act I, scene vi, lines 1–10, 11–20, and 21–30) of a monologue for Corneille's hero D. Rodrigue, caught in a horrible dilemma: he has discovered that the murderer of his father, whom he has sworn to avenge, is the father of the woman he loves ('Il faut venger un père ou perdre une maîtressê. . . . Père, maîtresse, honneur, amour!'). Charpentier's music, for *haute-contre* and continuo, is powerfully unified—by a consistent tonality (G is the tonic key throughout, though, strangely, the close turns suddenly to C) and by the use, in each song, of a common ritornello. Also, the overall structure is symmetrical: the outer airs are cast in an extremely meticulous and sensitive recitative

---

[2] This is my collective title; the three airs bear no titles, individually or collectively, in the *Mercure galant*.

—not even Lully was more respectful of textual rhythmic nuances—while the central air is a limpid, triple-time chaconne on a five-bar bass in G minor (a 'sérieux et magnifique' key, for Charpentier).

These are truly *airs sérieux*. In drastic contrast to them are Charpentier's *airs à boire*—five silly little bagatelles. The bawdiest—'Fenchon, la gentille Fenchon' ('Fanny, gentle Fanny')—survives in only one surprisingly late manuscript (1734); its beginning can suggest the patter-song prattle characteristic of these 'drinking songs' (Ex. 21). Much more successful, apparently, in Charpentier's time and well beyond (with versions in three manuscripts and two imprints), was *La Vieille* ('Beaux petits yeux d'écarlate'), which has a square-cut, popular-song-like melody and a satirical text reminiscent of Shakespeare's Sonnet 130 ('My mistress' eyes are nothing like the sun; | Coral is far more red than her lips' red'). Even more popular than *La Vieille*, and lastingly so, was a melody which Charpentier wrote for Molière's troupe, to replace the one

Ex. 21. 'Fenchon, la gentille Fenchon' (Cat. 454), *F-PN* MS Y 296(1), pp. 271–74, bars 1–11

(Fanny, kind Fanny, that Fanny we see on such fine Sundays.)

74

originally composed by Lully for Sganarelle's air in Act I, scene v, of *Le Médecin malgré lui*: 'Qu'ils sont doux, bouteille jolie, | . . . Vos petits glougloux!' (commonly known as 'L'Air des glougloux' (the Glug-glug Song)). Not only did Charpentier's tune remain in the repertoire of the Comédie-Française; it spawned a number of monophonic contrafacta. The earliest printed one of these transmuted the original into a bittersweet *air sérieux*, 'Qu'il est doux, charmante Climène', which was printed in 1717 in *La Clef des chansonniers: ou recueil des vaudevilles* . . . with a *timbre* (a caption above the song) indicating that 'L'air [est celui de] Qu'ils sont doux, bouteille mamie [*sic*]' (Ex. 22). (What is 'doux' in the parody is the masochistic pleasure the lover takes in Climène's rejections.) Moreover, the little air became part of the oral tradition, being used for a French-language version—'Un flambeau, Jeannette Isabelle!'—of a seventeenth-century Provençal *noël*; this in turn became—still with Charpentier's melody—the English carol 'Bring a torch, Jeanette Isabelle'.

Ex. 22. 'Qu'il est doux, charmante Climène' (Cat. 460), *La Clef des chansonniers* . . . (Paris: J.-B.-C. Ballard, 1717), i. 74–5

(How sweet it is, charming Climène, to feel
your blows! Fate would be full of jealousy
if you put an end to my misery. Ah! ah! ah!,
charming Climène, do go on not loving me!)

Cantatas

The eight works that are here called cantatas have in common only their being vocal compositions destined for performance as secular entertainment of some kind or other. None is actually termed a cantata by Charpentier, although they are all rooted in that genre of Italian secular chamber music.[3] This is most obviously true of the five compositions to Italian texts, but it is also true to some degree of the two French-language compositions and the one with a text in Latin.

Closest to Italian models are the modest cantatas (each no more than fifty bars long) *Superbo amore*, for soprano duet and continuo, and *Il mondo così va*, for solo soprano and continuo. They are found side by side in a late seventeenth-century French manuscript which contains other similar cantatas and arias by Italian composers. The longer *Beate mie pene*, also for soprano duo, is ingratiatingly rich in cantabile, *bel-canto*-style melodies. The still longer (190-bar) *Serenata a tre voci e simphonia*, for SAB trio, is also extremely Italianate—in melodic motifs, phrase-structure, harmony and tonal design, and handling of two-violin ritornellos. Its text is a litany of lessons in love, warning us, *Sú, sú, sú, non dormite. . . . Amor non vuole dormiglioso campion nelle sue schole* [*sic*] ('Up, up, up! no more sleeping! . . . Love wishes no sleep specialist in *his* schools'). Its music is lively and cute, its plan a shapely, symmetrical one: though through-composed, not strophic, its beginning and ending stanzas share similar melodic material and are assigned to the trio ensemble; in between, each of the three singers in turn is given a stanza's worth of solo opportunity.

The largest of the cantatas on Italian texts, about 350 bars long and scored very grandly for soloists, chorus, woodwinds, trumpets, timpani, strings, and continuo, is one in praise of the duke of Bavaria, brother-in-law of the Dauphin; belatedly, Charpentier added the word 'epithalamium' to its title, confirming the date of the work—or at least of its ultimate use—as 1685, when Maximilian II Emanuel, Elector of Bavaria, was married. The festival atmosphere of the piece, its pomp and magnificence, and even its mouthful of a title—*Epithalamio in lode dell'Altezza Serenissima Elettorale di Massimiliano Emanuel Duca di Baviera concento a cinque voci con stromenti*—all bespeak a

---

[3] Ironically, the term 'cantata' was applied contemporaneously to a work by Charpentier (and then at second hand), but for one whose music has not survived: *Le Roi d'Assyrie mourant*. This is cited by Le Cerf de la Viéville, who prints the texts of two airs from it, as a 'fragment . . . en espece de *Cantata*' (*Comparaison*, in Bourdelot and Bonnet, *Histoire*, iii. 33).

pièce d'occasion, undoubtedly commissioned from Charpentier by the Dauphin (who must have been pleased to have at hand a composer completely versed in Italian, both language and music, and to be able to offer brother-in-law and bride a gracious gift, very much *à la mode*: the electoral court in Munich was fashionably full of Italian theatre and church music and musicians). An opening call to attention, in the form of a big fanfare-filled tripartite prelude (A B A), gives way to stirring choruses, proud trios, and joyous solos, all rounded off by a *da capo* reprise of the opening chorus—and all full of Italian *vivacità*, not to mention gratuitous (but mellifluous) roulades in the best Scarlattian manner (Ex. 23).

Historically, the most important of the cantatas is *Orphée descendant aux enfers*: a work of 1683, it has been accepted as a precursor of the French cantatas which flowered in the early eighteenth century and described as the first 'genuine cantata in the French style'.[4] Without denying the historical priority of *Orphée* as the earliest extant cantata by a French composer, I would say, rather, than it is distinctly Italo-French in manner, and more of a dramatic *scena*, with an oratorio-like moralistic conclusion, than either the earlier Italian or the later French cantatas. An elegant and evocative work, even if it treats only a fragment of the Greek legend, it is scored very carefully for ATB trio, two violins, recorder, transverse flute, and continuo (bass viol and harpsichord). The instruments begin, with a slightly melancholy prelude dominated by the 'violon d'Orphée' (no lyre for him, at the hands of *this* Italianate Baroque-era composer!). Orpheus (an *haute-contre*, the part probably written for Charpentier himself) has a long, lamenting *récit*, heard by Ixion and Tantalus, two of the shades in Hades. (Not original with Charpentier: they appear in various versions of the myth.) They marvel at the beauty of Orpheus's singing, which has tempered their torments. Orpheus sings again of his grief. His auditors realize why he touches them so: he is a lover, and nothing equals love's sweetness, although—'Hélas, hélas!'—not even love can conquer all woes. With this they all agree, in an affecting final trio.

[4] David Tunley, *The Eighteenth-Century French Cantata* (London, 1974), 46–9, and Anthony, *French Baroque Music*, p. 360. Anthony later unearthed two cantata-like texts by Pierre Perrin (in his *Recueil de paroles de musique*), set by Etienne Moulinié and Jean Sablières, respectively, which must have antedated Charpentier's *Orphée* by almost twenty years; the music of these, however, is not extant. (Personal communication.)

(There are no more stars in the sky
than there are glories in thee!)

The other French cantata, 'Coulez, coulez, charmans ruis-seaux', attributed to 'M. Charpentier' in a manuscript at Avignon which cannot predate 1737, is of extremely doubtful authenticity as the work of *our* M. Charpentier, and in any case is of slight musical interest.[5]

Probably the most singular of Charpentier's compositions, certainly the most enigmatic, is the Latin cantata *Epitaphium Carpentarij*. (The first enigma about the work is the choice of a text in Latin for an essentially secular work. For what occasion, and under whose auspices, can it have been composed?) Like *Orphée descendant aux enfers*, 'Charpentier's Funeral Oration' is a quasi-dramatic work, in which the ghost of Charpentier appears to two mortal friends, Ignatius and Marcellus. (Why these names? Another enigma.) The composer recalls his earthly career with some bitterness.[6] Asked by the mortals about the music in heaven, he says that 'He who had the name Carissimi on earth is called Chaperon in heaven'—referring not only to his Roman mentor but suggesting, most puzzlingly, that the heavenly host mistakes Carissimi for François Chaperon—who, it will be recalled, was Charpentier's predecessor as *maître de musique* at the Sainte-Chapelle, holding the post from 1679 until his death in 1698. (There are surely puns here, on 'Carissimi'—*carissimi* means 'dear ones'—and 'Chaperon'—*capronus* means 'goat', with connotations of 'big, ugly goat'.) The ghost then prays for a celestial concert and is awarded one by 'trois anges qu'on entend et qu'on ne voit point'. Their lyrical 'Cantique des anges' (as the manuscript titles it) is truly celestial: the angels are a high-voice trio (SSA), and their accompaniment is not a basso continuo but an 'alto continuo'. Ignatius and Marcellus are enchanted with this melodious 'anti-Chaperonian' music. (Yet another enigma: why is the heavenly

---

[5] Anthony concludes that it is the work of 'one of the Avignon Charpentiers'; see his 'A Source for Secular Vocal Music in 18th Century Avignon: MS 1182 of the Bibliothèque du Muséum Calvet', *Acta musicologica*, 54 (1982), 261–79. This cantata is published, along with all the others by Charpentier except the *Epithalamio*, in Charpentier, *Vocal Chamber Music*, ed. John Powell (Madison, Wisconsin, 1986).

[6] See the epigraph of Chapter 1. Charpentier intensifies that rueful assessment by following it with this: *Et cum multo major numerus esset eorum qui me spernebant quam qui laudabant, musica mihi parvus honos sed magnum onus fuit; et, sicut ego nihil nascens intuli in hunc mundum, ita moriens nihil abstuli* ('And since those who scorned me were more numerous than those who lauded me, music became to me a very small honour and very onerous; and just as at my birth I brought nothing into the world, I took nothing from it at my death').

trio's lovely song—its text a conventionally dogmatic Trinitarian homily—heard as an attack on Chaperon?) Charpentier's shade urges his friends to 'repent and embrace this music of Chaperon' (but we have just been told it was *anti*-Chaperonian!): choose it 'as punishment and purgatory, and after death you will taste the joys of eternal life'. Charpentier's ghost and his two friends sing a final trio, its text a burst of punning slurs at the 'asinine, goatish detritus of Chaperon'.

A very puzzling composition indeed! but full of delicious musical touches, beginning with a unique, throbbing-bass prelude for the continuo that signifies the ghost's appearance and frightens Ignatius and Marcellus out of their wits; the former cries, 'What do I hear? What horrible-sounding roar, though similar to harmony, strikes my ears?' (Ex. 24).

Ex. 24. *Epitaphium Carpentarij* (Cat. 474), bars 1–14 (xiii. 60ᵛ)

Instrumental Chamber Works

Charpentier left less than a dozen secular instrumental works. A few of these, for full orchestra, may not seem appropriately classified as 'chamber' compositions. On the other hand, just as orchestral dances from Lully's operas or Lalande's ballets did double duty as background music for the King's evening meal (such as Lalande's *Symphonies pour le souper du Roi*), thus serving no longer as music for the theatre but music for the chamber, so too might Charpentier's orchestral pieces have served the Dauphin or Mlle de Guise.

Several of the works are miniatures or fragments: a pair of tiny minuets for paired recorders and continuo, a one-minute *Caprice pour trois violons* (the 'troisième' being a bass), a maddeningly fragmentary conclusion of a gigue (or chaconne) for bass viol, and a *Commencement d'ouverture pour ce que l'on voudra, en la rectifiant un peu*, abandoned after its first section had been composed. Another overture, apparently written similarly as a hedge against future need, *was* completed: the *Ouverture pour quelque belle entreprise, à cinq* (the number referring to the Lullian five-part scoring: G_1, C_1, C_2, C_3, and F_4).

A pair of triumphal 'airs de trompettes' from the early 1690s—a *Marche de triomphe pour les violons, trompettes, timbales, flûtes et hautbois* and a *Second air de trompettes, violons, flûtes, et hautbois et timbales*—are stirring processional pieces, much along the lines of the well-known prelude to the great D major Te Deum. Both are *rondeaux* with two *couplets*, the refrain being for the full orchestra, the *couplets* for trios—respectively flute/oboe pairs with continuo (specified as bass violin, bassoon, and organ) and two violins and continuo (without the bassoon). Charpentier is very explicit about the repetitions to be made: the form of both pieces is A A b A c A A (though the first 'air' may be extended by repeating yet again the sections from *couplet* 'b' on).

The most interesting and significant chamber pieces are a *Concert pour quatre parties de violes* and a *Sonate pour 2 flûtes allemandes, 2 dessus de violon, une basse de viole, une basse de violon à cinq cordes, un clavecin et un téorbe*. The *Concert* dates from 1680–1. The *Sonate* is not precisely datable: its manuscript, though an autograph, is not among Charpentier's 'mélanges autographes' and is undated; but circumstantial evidence, the handwriting, and the assured style invite a conjectural date in the mid-1680s. Thus we may have here the first French chamber suite conceived as an entity and the first piece of chamber music titled 'sonata' by a French composer.

Though the *Concert* may have some claim to historical primacy as a genuine suite, conceived as such, its scoring is oddly anachronistic, being that of an orchestra of viols in four parts, without basso continuo. (Solo-viol trios occasionally contribute some timbral nuances.) There are six movements. A 'learned' contrapuntal Prelude is to be played twice; it savours of French *fantaisies* of many years earlier (those of Etienne Moulinié, for example, if not of the even earlier Eustache Du Caurroy or Claude Le Jeune). The Prelude is followed by an untitled second movement in binary dance form (and close in style to the 'Allemande grave' among the *reposoir* pieces). Then comes a Sarabande *en rondeau* (Charpentier being explicit about the form, as in the *airs de trompettes*: A A b A c A A); both of its *couplets* are assigned to a trio of solo viols (SSB). A 'Gigue angloise' is then followed by a 'Gigue françoise'; to the ear the titles might well be reversed, for the 'Gigue angloise' has the dotted rhythms typical of the French gigue (or *loure*), while the 'Gigue françoise' is full of the stomping iambs of the British jig. (For reasons not at all clear, though the 'Gigue angloise' gets but a single run-through, the 'Gigue françoise' is to be played three times.) The *Concert* concludes with a Passecaille, which is rounded off at the end by a return of its 'première ritornelle' (its first section)—a procedure occasionally found in other works by Charpentier, as we have seen, and in fact one commonly found in chaconnes or passecailles by his French contemporaries.

In the *Sonate* à 8, Charpentier combines elements of sonata and suite (as Couperin was to do in *Les Nations* many years later). Three of the nine movements are sonata-like in not being dance-related: the opening preludial 'Grave', the following 'Récit de la basse de viole', and a parallel 'Récit de la basse de violon' (the fourth movement). The other movements are named dances: Sarabande (the third movement), Bourrée, Gavotte, Gigue, Passecaille, and Chaconne (fifth through ninth movements). The *récits* are clearly intended to show off their respective foreground instruments; the bass-violin *récit* is truly a virtuoso piece, with much élan (Ex. 25).

Ex. 25. *Sonate* [à 8] (Cat. 548), 'Récit de la basse de violon', bars 7–9
(*F-Pn* Vm⁷ 4813)

The confidence mastery of writing for instrumental ensemble
revealed by the *Concert* and the *Sonate* cannot help but leave us
regretful that, because of the nature of his employment and
employers, Charpentier had virtually no opportunity to display it
often—except in his theatrical music, to which we now turn.

V
MUSIC FOR THE THEATRE

La Conversation. De grace, de grace, encore cette courante!
La Musique. C'est un menuet, un menuet, ignorante!

Charpentier, *Les Plaisirs de Versailles*

CHARPENTIER wrote music for the theatre during most of his career, from the early 1670s to the mid-1690s. He was approached in 1672 by Molière, as we have seen, to write music for Molière's Troupe du Roi, and continued to compose for the company until the mid-1680s. He also seems to have written theatrical music at the instigation of the Grand Dauphin. For Mlle de Guise, too, and for the Jesuit Collège Louis-le-Grand he wrote a number of theatre pieces; other works, their music no longer extant, are cited in the *Mercure galant* and by Titon du Tillet. Charpentier's last work for the lyric theatre, it would seem, was the tragedy *Médée*, produced at the Opéra in 1693. Thus, although one rightly tends to think of him as primarily a church musician, Charpentier was a productive and versatile composer for the stage as well, and a considerable body of dramatic music by him is extant. It consists of two groups of compositions: overtures, *intermèdes*, and incidental music for stage plays, and self-contained musico-dramatic entertainments: pastorales, operatic divertissements, and *tragédies en musique*.

Music for Stage Plays

In the last quarter of the seventeenth century not only did music pervade the nearly dead *ballet de cour*, the declining *comédie-ballet*, and the emerging *tragédie lyrique*; all kinds of other stage works were full of incidental music—orchestral overtures and dances; solo *récits* and *airs*; pieces for duos, trios, and other vocal ensembles; and even choruses. Moreover, *intermèdes*—entr'acte musical entertainments (most often farcical or pastoral irrelevancies, but diverting ones)—were commonly interpolated in all types of stage plays except the most classic of classic tragedies. Charpentier wrote a considerable amount of such music for the theatre, virtually all of it for the Comédie-Française—that is, for the troupe that came to be called the Comédie-Française in 1680, having earlier been known as Molière's troupe, the Comédiens du Roi.[1]

When Molière and Lully parted company in 1672, the actor-playwright immediately turned to Charpentier as his new collaborator. Molière's one-act comedy *La Comtesse d'Escarbagnas* had been premièred at court on 2 December 1671, serving as an introduction to the *Ballet des ballets*, a pastiche put together from works with music by Lully; but when the comedy was first performed publicly in Paris (8 July 1672) it was preceded by an overture by Charpentier and followed by a revival of *Le Mariage forcé*, with new *intermèdes* composed by him as well as ballet music for new dances. The surviving manuscript score, apparently complete, consists of the *Ouverture de la Comtesse d'Escarbagnas* followed by a dozen other pieces, both vocal and instrumental. No scenario exists, however, to tell us exactly how or where these fitted into the comedies or the 'nouveaux intermèdes', and in fact it is not completely clear which pieces belong to which play (apart from the overture, of course).

One amusing sequence of these pieces (Cat. 494 (9–11)), which probably was the heart of the last 'new intermezzo' for *Le Mariage forcé*, typifies the most common sort of farcical *intermède* of the time. A 'Trio grotesque' of self-styled musicians (*haute-contre*, tenor, and bass, with continuo) bounces onstage; they introduce themselves:

> La, la, la, la, . . .
>   Bonjour pour trente mille années,
> Chers compagnons, puisqu'icy nous voilà—
> Trois favoris d'ut, re, mi, fa, sol, la.
>   Qu'icy nos voix soient desguesnées:
>   Chantons!

[1] For a more detailed account than is possible here, see H. W. Hitchcock, 'Marc-Antoine Charpentier and the Comédie-Française', *Journal of the American Musicological Society*, 24 (1971), 256–81.

La, la, la, la, . . .
  Good day for thirty thousand years,
  Dear companions, for here we are—
Three favourites of doh, ray, me, fah, soh, lah.
  Let our voices be unleashed:
      Let's sing!

They tickle themselves (and us) with patter-song babbling, nonsense-syllable gabbling ('tic toc, chic choc, nic noc, fric froc . . .'), and mock-honorific salutations to *commedia dell'arte* characters ('le seigneur Gratian . . . le seigneur Arlequin . . . le seigneur Pantalon'). They do a dance number ('Les Grotesques'). They finally essay a 'joli concert', inviting the participation of 'des chiens, des chats et des rossignols d'Arcadie'. It pleases *them*, at least:

      O la belle symphonie!
      Qu'elle est douce, qu'elle a d'appas!

      O what a pretty concert!
      How sweet, how enticing it is!

This they cry, along with sounds imitating the dogs, cats, and 'Arcadian nightingales'—donkeys (Ex. 26).

  The Grotesques say, with little exaggeration, *Point de rime et point de raison | Tout est bon quoi qu'on die | Tout bruit forme mélodie* ('No rhyme or reason at all— | No matter what we say, it will do: | Any noise will make a tune'). This sort of clever

Ex. 26. *Intermède nouveau du Mariage forcé* (Cat. 494 (11), bars 33–56 (xvi. 45–45ᵛ)

nonsense, farce, and fantasy—often semi-improvised, as in the *commedia dell'arte* (and the 'Italian business', as here, was not uncommon)—is the very stuff of many of the *intermèdes*, which, it was hoped, would outdo in amusement the very comedies in which they were interpolated.

Charpentier's first major work for Molière was the score for *Le Malade imaginaire* of early 1673, which includes such comic *intermèdes* to go after Acts I and II and, at the end of the play, the hilarious *Cérémonie des médecins*, besides a 'petit opéra impromptu' for the characters Cléante and Angélique in Act II, scene v. (Charpentier also composed an overture and set completely to music Molière's lengthy prologue, an allegorical pastorale unrelated to the comedy but full of shepherds and shepherdesses, satyrs and zephyrs—and also panegyrics of Louis XIV, Molière having hoped that the King would invite him, as usual, to present the work's première at court.)

The Premier Intermède, between Acts I and II, is sheer buffoonery, a polyglot song-and-dance playlet owing much to the *commedia dell'arte*: Polichinelle (the Neapolitan comedy's Pulcinella) serenades his mistress with the Italian song 'Nott'e dì'; he gets a response—not from his Toinette, however, but from an old woman, who sings the burlesque canzonetta 'Zerbinetti'. His remonstrances are interrupted by fiddlers and dancers; he is arrested and beaten by the Night Watch, but finally released thanks to a bribe he offers. The Second Intermède is an exotic, carnivalesque masquerade offered as entertainment to the 'malade imaginaire' by his brother, who explains near the close of Act II what is in store for them: 'Egyptiens, vêtus en Mores, qui font des danses mêlées de chansons, où je suis sûr que vous prendrez plaisir.' (The 'gypsies costumed as moors' not only sing and dance but carry monkeys, which they make leap about in one of the dance *entrées*.)

The 'Ceremony of Doctors' is a macaronic mixture of farce and savage satire of the medical profession—not, strictly speaking, an *intermède* at all but rather, like the *Ballet des nations* of *Le Bourgeois gentilhomme* (1670, to music by Lully), the climactic finale of the play proper. Charpentier's score for it follows Molière's text exactly, after beginning with a properly pompous overture, a sprightly orchestral dance for the decorators ('Les Tapissiers') who are to prepare the hall, and a solemn processional march for the entrée of the Faculty of Medicine, assembled to feign conferring a medical doctorate on the hypochondriac. Instrumental ensemble and 'chorus' (six singers are named in the manuscript) deliver the mock applause of 'Bene, bene respondere'; at the mock praise of 'Vivat, vivat, cent fois vivat' they are augmented by apothecaries' mortars and pestles (ingeniously treated as orchestral instruments and scored in two parts, high and low, like timpani). Surgeons and apothecaries romp through a short *air de ballet*; they are joined by the doctors, and all march out of the hall to the chorus of the 'grand Vivat'.

Le Malade imaginaire was Molière's last play (he died after the fourth performance). It was also the first to suffer under Lully's monopolistic machinations against the Troupe du Roi and other presumptive competitors for the audiences of his Académie Royale de Musique, the Opéra. The six singers named in Charpentier's manuscript add up to precisely the number to which theatre troupes in Paris were limited under a royal ordinance obtained by Lully in August 1672; and we can be sure that, reflecting the same ordinance, the 'orchestra' of the première numbered no more than twelve players. By April 1673 Lully had tightened his grip still further, with a new ordinance stipulating that no more than two singers and six *violons* (that is, string players) could be used by companies other than the Académie de Musique. (From this date on, the 'orchestra' for the musical numbers of the Comédie-Française, as Charpentier scores for it, consisted of two *dessus de violon*, one each of *haute-contre*, *taille*, and *basse de violon*, and harpsichord. His scores, which resonate so richly at the hands of a good-sized chamber orchestra, were in fact realized by a sextet.)

The first music Charpentier seems to have revised for the troupe under the April 1673 ordinance was that for *Le Malade imaginaire*. Calling the revision '*Le Malade imaginaire avec les défenses*' (. . . under the bans), he wrote a new overture and composed as a simple *air en rondeau* a new and much less elaborate prologue—a brief jibe at the medical fraternity, for a shepherdess afflicted with lovesickness: *Votre plus haut savoir n'est que pure chimère* ('Your most profound knowledge is naught but pure sham'). He also revised the *intermèdes*, though perhaps not the *Cerémonie des médecins*. About a decade later (in late 1685 or early 1686), under yet another crushingly restrictive ordinance

89

(according to which the troupe could use as singers only two *actors* already in its employ), Charpentier had to re-revise his score, which he now titled, probably with exasperation, '*Le Malade imaginaire* rajusté autrement pour la 3ème fois'.[2]

Between the first and third versions of his music for *Le Malade imaginaire*, Charpentier was kept quite busy by the Comédie-Française, revising or replacing the music of earlier plays to conform with the royal ordinances and composing scores for new ones. Among the latter, the most important are the five-act tragicomedy *Circé* (March 1675, with a text by Thomas Corneille) and the three-act comedy *Les Fous divertissants* (November 1680; text by Raymond Poisson). Charpentier also wrote completely new scores for revivals of two older plays. One, brought back in 1682 after more than thirty years, was Pierre Corneille's *Andromède*, a *tragédie à machines* which originally had humdrum music, by the poet–musician called Dassoucy, intended merely 'to satisfy the ears of the spectators while the eyes are engaged watching the descent or ascent of a machine'.[3] The other, revived in 1685, was Donneau de Visé's *Les Amours de Vénus et d'Adonis* of 1670.

Circé was an elaborate work 'orné de machines, de changements de théâtre, et de musique' and a considerable success, with some forty performances in the six months following its opening and, in 1676, publication of a volume of *Airs de la comédie de Circé* by the prestigious music publishers Ballard. Not only did *Circé* have a prologue fully composed by Charpentier (complete with opening overture); the play itself was full of music—many dances, vocal solos, and ensembles of up to five parts. The overture is clearly based on Lully's models but expands interestingly their stereotyped form: the first section adds to the usual march (in 2 metre) a gigue in 6/4; then comes the expected 'fugue'—which is not, however, repeated as usual but instead is followed by a reprise of the gigue (so the form of the whole is ‖: a :‖ b c b). The orchestral *airs de ballet*—all

---

[2] All of Charpentier's music for *Le Malade imaginaire* (except for the original Premier Intermède and the 'petit opéra' of Act II) is published in *Prologues et intermèdes du Malade imaginaire de Molière*, ed. H. W. Hitchcock (Geneva, 1973). Charpentier's music for the Premier Intermède and that for Act II, scene v, was later rediscovered by John Powell, who discusses it (along with the complex history of the entire score) in 'Charpentier's Music for Molière's *Le Malade imaginaire* and its Revisions', *Journal of the American Musicological Society*, 39 (1986), 87–142.

[3] As translated in Anthony, *French Baroque Music*, p. 61.

scored for a four-part string group, as is the overture (the G1, S1, S2, F4 combination favoured by Charpentier)—are brilliant and buoyant, especially a majestic 'Prélude pour faire entrer les Arts et les Plaisirs' (the allegorical characters of the Prologue), with rich dark harmonies and an especially deep bass line which explores the lowest range (down to great B) of the French *basse de violon*; and a splendid Passecaille (*en rondeau*, like so many French passecailles and chaconnes of the period) which is of a remarkable contrapuntal vitality, its *parties de remplissage*—those inner voices legendarily left by Lully to be filled in by assistants—as shapely and with as much melodic integrity as the *dessus* and *basse* lines.[4] Of particular interest are several vocal numbers with indications in Charpentier's manuscript for participation (or not) of dancers: 'Tous . . . danseurs . . . sans danseurs . . . danseurs . . . tous'; others in which he cues their movements ('Les sauteurs courent . . . figure placée . . . elle se deffait'); and one, 'Les Pantomimes', in which he cues their emotional expressions and gestures ('Marques d'obéissance . . . Joye . . . Complaisance . . . Colère—et tendresse . . . Rage—et pitié . . . fureur et promptitude').

Poisson's comedy *Les Fous divertissants*—which might be translated 'The Amusing Crazies'—had its first run in Paris in the fall of 1680. The play is frothy and insubstantial, Charpentier's *intermèdes* equally so but full of musical wit. The two—play and entr'acte episodes—are constantly being conflated in a crazy hodgepodge, the characters of the comedy getting all mixed up with the 'musiciens amoureux' and the 'fous avec leurs marottes' (foolscaps) of the *intermèdes*. (Probably the best-known counterpart in the modern repertoire is Strauss's *Ariadne auf Naxos*—which parodies, of course, the couplings of legitimate and lyric, serious and comic genres in the theatre of the *grand siècle*.) Two musical numbers stand out, the Premier Intermède, concluding Act I, in which two musicians (*haute-contre* and bass) plead with two of the comedy's characters to bring them luck in love ('Hélas, hélas! nous nous plaignons tous deux | Serions-nous amoureux?'), and the Second Intermède, between Acts II and III, which has a very funny Laughers' Trio ('Trio des rieurs') for three serenading musicians—it begins, 'Ha, ha, ha, ha, ha, ha,

---

[4] The Passecaille is published as part of a hypothetical reconstruction of the Premier Intermède of *Le Malade imaginaire*, included among the *Prologues et intermèdes du Malade imaginaire* cited in n. 2.

ha, ha, ha, ha, ha, ha . . .'—to which onlooking 'dancing crazies'—*fous dansants*—are to clap their hands in rhythm, then dance rings around the singers.

The Comédie-Française revised Corneille's *Andromède* extensively for the 1682 revival; it turned out to be fabulously expensive because of intricate and marvellous new machines (one of which bore a live horse simulating the flight of the winged Pegasus, with the actor playing Perseus astride it). The company decided to scrap Dassoucy's original score, and Charpentier redid the entire thing. His extensive music begins with a fine Lullian overture (scored à 4, however, and without a hint of instruments other than strings) and music for a lengthy new prologue. Then, in each act, there are musical numbers— solo airs, dialogues, and 'choruses' (for those members of the troupe who could sing)—and, as *intermèdes*, orchestral *airs de ballet* (no playlets or comic turns admitted to this tragedy). The music for these dances is delectable: A Sarabande *en rondeau* serves as the Premier Intermède (between Acts I and II); the Second, 'Les Vents', is an extremely unusual character-piece, with hurricane-force strings rushing about madly, in a time signature—2/4—almost never found in Charpentier's (or Lully's) music, hence undoubtedly signifying something unusual, probably an especially fast tempo (Ex. 27). Between Acts III and IV comes a 'Caprice', an attractively contrapuntal, canzona-like movement; and, between Acts IV and V, a 'Premier air' featuring exceptional changes of metre (¢ 3 ¢ 3 ¢) is followed by a 'Second air' (a 'Gigue angloise' similar to the one in the *Concert pour quatre parties de violes*).

Much less successful than *Andromède* (with only four performances) was Donneau de Visé's tragedy *Les Amours de Vénus et d'Adonis*, as revived in 1685 with additions in the form of elaborate music by Charpentier—overture, long prologue, and four *intermèdes*. The mythological figures of the play inspired, for these musical interludes, neither farcical *intermèdes* nor *airs de ballet* but bucolic pastoral scenes populated by gentle shepherds and shepherdesses. But not even De Visé himself (wearing his hat as editor of the *Mercure galant*) had much to say for the production, except to remark that it included 'une plainte qui a charmé tous ceux qui l'ont entendue et qui se connaissent en musique'. This 'Plainte de la bergère' ('Nymphes, ne songez plus qu'à répandre des larmes') is indeed a fine, affecting

example of the genre; 130 bars long, with ritornellos for strings à 4, it ends up as a big *air en rondeau* with a central recitative (A b A)—or perhaps the term *da capo aria* would be equally appropriate, for the moody, chromatically coloured lament proper (the A section) is warmly Italianate, with melting melismas on the word *larmes* ('tears'), though the brief mid-passage is definitively, declamatorily French. Charpentier seems to have lavished special effort on this final *air* (it is followed, among these *intermèdes*, only by a 'Caprice' for the strings 'to be played until Act V [begins]'): he even composed, for the strings, two versions of a prelude for it (carefully preserving both). Earlier, in the 'Intermède du 3ᵉ au 4ᵉ acte', there had appeared a 'Menuet pour la bergère', an *air* with a second stanza elaborated as a *double* (unique among Charpentier's works). Example 28 gives the end of each stanza, to suggest how the old technique of

93

Ex. 28. *Les Amours de Vénus et d'Adonis* (Cat. 507 (10)), *double*,
bars 25–40 (*dessus* only), 1st and 2nd stanzas) (xxii. 26ᵛ–27, 31ᵛ)

(What is the point of these mortal troubles, and of
life with nothing but sighs? Love should avoid
such grief: it exists only for pleasure.)

elaborate melodic variation in the *doubles* of *airs de cour* had been
smoothed out under the influence of Italian *bel canto*.

Operatic Entertainments

Only after Lully died in 1687 did Charpentier gain entry—six
years later—to the Académie Royale de Musique (the Opéra),
where his *Médée* was produced. However, during the 1680s, if

94

not earlier, he had composed the music for a number of other operatic works: seven or eight for Mlle de Guise; two, on courtly subjects, if not specifically for the Dauphin, perhaps commissioned through his influence; two sacred tragedies for the Jesuits' Collège Louis-le-Grand; and several stage pieces whose music has not survived, plus others which are incomplete.[5] Also identified as by Charpentier are two *pastoralette* on Italian texts in a late-seventeenth-century French manuscript (not in Charpentier's hand). Space limitations do not permit a lengthy discussion of each of these works, some of which are extremely long and complex; it may be useful to treat them here by genre—pastorale, operatic divertissement, and lyric tragedy.

Pastorales

The French penchant for pastoral drama during the *grand siècle* is well known, and has been mentioned earlier. Though the very existence of the pastorale was threatened by the rise of French classical drama, its traditional characters—not only shepherds and shepherdesses but nymphs and satyrs, deities and devils, sorcerers and buffoons, magicians and monsters—were simply too attractive as dramatic raw material to be given up, and they continued to populate the scenes of many kinds of stage works (if not classical tragedies), including of course the pastorale proper. This is reflected faithfully in Charpentier's compositions for the theatre, which include more pastorales than any other genre. Of the dramatic compositions he wrote for Mlle de Guise, only two are not pastorales—*Les Arts florissants* (which Charpentier specifically calls an 'opéra') and *La Descente d'Orphée aux enfers* (its two extant acts seeming to be on their way to a complete *tragédie en musique*). One of the two courtly dramatic works—*Le Fête de Rueil*—is a pastorale. The *Pastoralette*

[5] The lost works include a 'petit opéra', *Les Amours d'Acis et de Galatée*, cited in the *Mercure galant* of November 1678 and 'un opéra intitulé *Philomèle*' (with some parts composed by the Duc d'Orléans) which Titon du Tillet claims had three performances at the Théâtre du Palais-Royal. He also speaks of another dramatic work called *Le Retour du printemps* and a third, *Le Jugement de Pan*, which is identified in the 'Mémoire des ouvrages de . . . Mr Charpentier' drawn up by his nephew in 1726 as the *Petite pastorale* (the manuscript of which is incomplete). (The 'Mémoire . . .' is discussed and partially reproduced in Hitchcock, 'Charpentier: Mémoire and Index'.) The music of *Celse Martyr*, *tragédie en musique*, composed for the Jesuits in 1687, is lost, though a libretto survives; and the manuscript of only two acts of *La Descente d'Orphée aux enfers*, composed for Mlle de Guise, has come down to us.

italiane are by definition pastorales. And shepherds and shepherdesses even make an appearance in the two great tragedies *David et Jonathas* and *Médée*.

The earliest pastoral drama Charpentier composed for the musicians of Mlle de Guise seems to have been *Actéon: Pastorale en musique*, which dates from 1683–5; he later reworked it slightly, titling the revision *Actéon changé en biche*. Its source is the Ovidian legend of the metamorphosis of the hunter Actaeon into a stag at the order of Diana, chaste goddess of the hunt, who while bathing with her sisters had been viewed by him, and of his being killed by his own dogs and those of his fellow hunters (*Metamorphoses*, iii. 138 ff). Following a French overture à la Charpentier (‖: a :‖ b c, the 'b' section being a merry minuet, the 'c' being fugal) and a programmatic fanfare ('Bruit de chasse'), the work unfolds in a single act, with six scenes. It has principal roles for Actéon (*haute-contre*) and Diana (soprano), minor roles for three 'Nymphs of Diana' and Juno (who appears late in the work to announce Actaeon's death to his companions), a Chorus of Hunters, and a Chorus of Nymphs of Diana. As in the other works for Mlle de Guise, the instrumental requirements are not great (pairs of recorders and treble viols, bass viol, and harpsichord), but the instruments have an important role in movements clearly (and cleverly) included to allow for stage business—the opening 'Sounds of the Hunt', a minuet, a gavotte *en rondeau*, and most notably a long C minor 'Plainte' as Actaeon views with consternation his transformed image in the waters of a forest pool. (It must have been thought *too* long: for the revised version, Charpentier cut it from 101 bars to 41.) The best word for the vocal music of this pastorale is 'charming', although the lament of the final hunters' chorus goes beyond being merely charming.

For another pastorale for Mlle de Guise, Charpentier turned back to some very early music of his: that for the original prologue of Molière's *Le Malade imaginaire* (which had gone unperformed, since the première at court hoped for by Molière had never taken place). The libretto of *La Couronne de fleurs* (1685), in three scenes, is a close adaptation of Molière's rather elegant if stilted poetic prologue, full of fashionable twelve-syllable alexandrines, with the original characters and plot line being retained. These add up, to today's taste, to a strange pastiche in which fanciful pastoral figures (the goddess Flore, the god Pan, the shepherdesses Rosalie, Amaranthe, and Hyacinthe, the shepherds Forestan, Sylvandre, and Mirtil) busy themselves mouthing plaudits and praise of Louis XIV. The flower-crown of the title is a prize promised by Flore to whichever shepherd or shepherdess best sings the glorious exploits of the royal conqueror who has put an end to wars and weeping. After each has given it a try, Pan appears, demanding that they cease their presumptuous contest: not even Apollo with his lyre would dare attempt to describe the glories of the incomparable Sun King. They fall silent. Flore, however, rewards them all, giving to each some blossoms from the crown, and all eight characters join in song, hoping that, just as Louis is 'master of the world', so may he also become 'master of time' and enjoy the flowers of a hundred springtimes:

> Puisse le grand Louis l'honneur des conquérants,
>   Comme il est du monde le maître,
>   Devenir le maître du temps,
> Et voir à cent hivers succéder le printemps.

Charpentier does what he can with this material, enlivening with occasional word-painting roulades the rigorously observed alexandrines and octameters of the verses. Perhaps it was his idea, too, to follow each of the shepherds' solos with a pleasantly contrasting variant of it for all the singers, and to write, for the instruments (a pair of obbligato viols and unspecified continuo), several little *symphonies* to which the singers probably danced. However, except for Pan, who has some characterful 'anger' music, all is quite bland and colourless.

Even more monochromatic, perhaps understandably, is an *Idyle sur le retour de la santé du Roi*, composed for the Hôtel de Guise in late 1686 or very early 1687. This was one of many works offered up in Paris and elsewhere in celebration of Louis XIV's recovery from a life-threatening operation. (One was the Te Deum of Lully, who wounded his foot while conducting it with a heavy staff-like baton and died from the gangrene that developed.) The theme of the *Idyle . . .*, as one of the shepherds puts it (in a carefully constructed alexandrine with perfectly balanced hemistiches), is 'Louis ne souffre plus, nos malheurs sont finis'. The pastorale is in every respect a *pièce d'occasion*, with an embarrassingly maudlin text and no dramatic tension whatever. For the undifferentiated group of nine 'bergers et bergères' (who occasionally dance to the tunes of two treble viols or recorders and continuo) Charpentier wrote a determinedly cheerful score—one, we might say, with a frozen smile.

Il faut rire et chanter: dispute de bergers (1684–5), also for Mlle de Guise's musicians, is more sharply drawn—partly because the 'dispute' is so simple, the participants in it at such opposite poles of feeling. A chorus called, delightfully, 'Chœur de bergers et de bergères aimants rire'—seven singers, two each for the soprano and bass parts, one each for low soprano (*bas-dessus*), *haute-contre*, and tenor parts—is deplored by a Shepherd of Sorrow ('Berger chagrin'). He is a joyless grump who urges them to face up to the fact that mortal life is full of unhappiness, and always will be; they should stop laughing and singing and dancing. But with the help of 'Pâtres jouants des instruments'—were the few accompanying musicians costumed and onstage?—the group finally persuades him otherwise, in a typically French campaign of 'strength through joy' propaganda: his last line is, in fact, 'Oui, de tous maux la joie est le contrepoison!' This is another 'charming' pastorale, but with well-projected contrasts between the joyful shepherds and the 'Berger chagrin'—their music consistently light, bright, vivacious, and dance-related; his, mainly dark, minor-modal, slower-moving, and more abstract. Though relatively long (more than seven hundred bars), *Il faut rire et chanter* has but one scene; it unrolls, however (after a miniature French overture), rather like a comic strip, in compact blocks of energetic, characterful, contrasting sub-scenes.

Perhaps it was Mlle de Guise's piety that led to two pastorales by Charpentier on the Christmas story. One is the attractive if slight and relatively undramatic *Sur la naissance de Notre Seigneur Jésus Christ: Pastorale*. The other, much broader-gauged, more colourful, and more lovingly composed, is the similarly titled *Pastorale sur la naissance de Notre Seigneur Jésus Christ*. As we noted earlier, the pastoral aspects of the Christmas story—the shepherds in the fields of Judea, the infant in the manger surrounded by farm animals—were emphasized by Charpentier in some dramatic motets; here are similarly oriented Christmastide works, but composed on French texts and staged in private chambers.

Sur la naissance . . . is built in two counterbalanced scenes. In Scene 1 we are in the stable at Bethlehem: the pastoral couple

Silvie and Tircis gaze at the crèche, at first chattering earnestly about the charm of the Child, the noble humility of the Virgin Mother, and the benign bemusement of Joseph, then duetting rapturously on the Lord's bounty. In Scene 2 we are in the hills of Judea: Silvie and Tircis have returned to reassure their companions that all is well: the Shepherd of shepherds is in the crib, Messiah is born. All take up their musettes and, to the music of a sarabande, sing joyously, 'No more sadness, no more sighs!'

The second, larger 'noël français' (as Charpentier refers to the *Pastorale sur la naissance* . . .) is on an altogether different level of accomplishment and artistry; it must be classed among the composer's finest works. He had, to begin with, a text of exceptional poetic quality and dramatic potential; to it he responded with music of consistent inspiration and craftsmanship. Each of the six scenes is of a chiselled, cameo-like perfection— but also of a driving dramatic energy. The locale shifts interestingly, from the Judean shepherds' meadows to the empyrean (where angelic choirs rejoice in the newborn Lord) and then to the stable in Bethlehem. The characters are firmly moulded: Shepherds and Shepherdesses (chorus à 5), who respond sensitively to each new development in the drama; a solemn, wise Elder among them ('L'Ancien', a baritone); a silver-voiced annunciant Angel (soprano); an appropriately celestial Angelic Choir (SSSA, with 'alto continuo'). The music is exceptionally well worked and expressive; word-painting abounds, but always subordinate to precise text declamation and general affect. Typical is the melodiously arched yet perfectly declaimed recitative with which Charpentier sets the Elder's slightly hesitant, awe-struck reaction to first seeing the Child (Ex. 29): 'l'homme-dieu' appropriately gets the highest notes, 'l'ange' the next-highest, 'notre misère' the lowest; the division between the two quatrains of the text is carefully underlined by a cadence and a punctuating rest at 'misère'; the rising sequential repetition of 'Ainsi nous l'a marqué' subtly emphasizes the old man's amazement at actually witnessing the materialization of the Angel's promise. Impressive in another way is the contrapuntal skill underlying the jubilant, not to say tintinnabulary, carolling of the Angelic Choir ('Glory without end! eternal glory!')—with the *haute-contre* stretching out 'éternelle' over five bars) and the lilting, swooping 'Petit air de violes' which follows (Ex. 30).

99

Ex. 29. *Pastorale sur la naissance de Notre Seigneur Jésus Christ*, revision of Part II (Cat. 483a), bars 1–8 (xxii. 32)

(Happy shepherds, here is the place where
God-made-man, assuming our miserable
state, has just been born— exactly as the
all-powerful angel indicated to us.)

Perhaps upon the recommendation of the Dauphin, Charpentier was commissioned in 1685 to write the music for a pastorale to be performed at the château in the town of Rueil, near Paris, of Armand-Jean du Plessis de Vignerot, duc de Richelieu, descendant and namesake of the famous cardinal (who had built the château, with its elaborate gardens). The duke wished to honour Louis XIV by erecting a statue of him in the gardens, and hoped to persuade the ruler to attend a fête centred on its unveiling.[6] A highlight of the fête was to be a *pastorale en musique*—Charpentier's setting of *La Fête de Rueil*. There is no clue, in Charpentier's manuscript, as to what or whose musicians were to be hired or borrowed for the performance,

[6] I am grateful to Patricia Ranum for having shared with me, prior to its publication, her account of the planning and preparations for this event.

but the scoring à 5 for the *tous* passages, and the instrumentation —recorders and transverse flutes, oboes, bassoon, violins, other strings, and harpsichord—suggest those of the Dauphin. Whether the pastorale was ever performed is uncertain, since the King could not come as hoped, and the *Mercure galant*'s report of the lesser festivities that did take place does not mention any musical divertissement. The work is not without

Ex. 30. *Pastorale sur la naissance de Notre Seigneur Jésus Christ* (Cat. 483), bars 535–56 (xxi. 67ᵛ)

sence im - mor - tel - le;　　　lou - ange à ja - mais à l'es - sence im - mor - tel -

sence im - mor - tel - le;　　　lou - ange à ja - mais à l'es - sence im - mor - tel -

sence im - mor - tel - le;　lou - ange à ja - mais, à ja - mais à l'es - sence im - mor - tel–

sence im - mor - tel - le;　lou - ange à ja - mais, à ja - mais à l'es - sence im - mor - tel -

Dessus
de violon

Dessus
de violon

le.

le.

le.

le.

(Eternal glory, glory without end, [and] in the
heavens praise forever, praise to the immortal Being.)

interest and attractiveness, although its text is topical in the
extreme, as we might expect—full of lauds for Louis and even
mention of the cardinal (whose centennial birth year it was).
Lyricism and lightness pervade the vocal music throughout,
side-by-side with tripping dances. In the seventh and final
scene, Pan, god of shepherds, appears, to comment that,
although he has observed more than fifty kings, never has he
known one such as Louis XIV—never such a 'maître de victoire
ni plus amoureux dè la paix'. This evokes a paroxysm of
praises from the assembled shepherds, shepherdesses, and
satyrs—a long set of choruses shot through with *petit-chœur*
trios, orchestral ritornellos, and ballet numbers. No wonder
Charpentier's nephew, in his 'Mémoire' of the composer's works

(the scores of which he had inherited), characterized this pastorale as 'Prélude, grand concert pour le roi défunt, ballets, &c'.

Operatic Divertissements

Two stage works by Charpentier may best be termed 'operatic divertissements': *Les Plaisirs de Versailles* (from the early 1680s) and *Les Arts florissants* (1685-6). These are sung throughout, in the manner of opera (and, as mentioned, Charpentier actually subtitled *Les Arts florissants* 'opéra'), yet, unlike operas of the time, each is in only a single act (of five and four scenes, respectively); *Les Arts . . .* lasts about three-quarters of an hour, *Les Plaisirs . . .* 'une heure et demie' (says Charpentier in the manuscript). As allegorical fantasies, they relate to the divertissements that lighten the acts of Lully's (and Charpentier's) *tragédies lyriques*: they both treat the arts and other leisure-time pleasures ('La Musique' having a leading role in each). Both dutifully bow and scrape to Louis XIV, but lightly, not in such fulsome platitudes as to discourage performances today.

Charpentier's nephew claims that *Les Plaisirs de Versailles* was a 'pièce pour les appartements du Roi'—for those evening entertainments at Versailles hosted by the King and called generically 'the apartments'. Perhaps so: the King is addressed directly at the very end of the work. The scene, in any case, according to Charpentier's manuscript, is 'dans les app[artements]', and the dialogue revolves around the sorts of pleasures enjoyed by the courtiers during such evenings— music, conversation, gastronomy, games, and the like. The principal characters are La Musique and La Conversation, together with a Chœur des Plaisirs; Comus ('God of Festivities') and Le Jeu (Games) appear half-way through. Music's singing is interrupted by Conversation, who cannot stop prattling. They argue at length and with increasing heat: which of them is more essential to pleasure? Fearful that they will both leave the château in a huff, the Chorus of Pleasures calls on Comus to mediate. He offers the quarrellers cocoa, fine wine, pastries— but to no avail; they persist in their bickering. He pleads for help to Le Jeu, who is equally unsuccessful. Somehow, though, the two are finally reconciled, and the Chorus of Pleasures sighs in relief: both music and conversation—'nos flûtes et nos voix'—can still help distract the *grand Roi* from his martial labours.

This is lightweight fluff, to be sure. All the more striking, then, is the sharpness with which Charpentier limns each character musically. La Musique is languid, tender, sensuous; Conversation has to admit she is a 'sociable sirène'. Conversation is a non-stop chatterbox (and something of a featherhead: she cannot tell a minuet from a courante); Music allows, though, that she is a 'babillarde divinité'. Comus, a bass, is a gourmand of small sensibility and Falstaffian bluster; Le Jeu, an *haute-contre*, a wheedling card-sharp. Example 31 offers typical passages from the music for each.

Ex. 31. *Les Plaisirs de Versailles* (Cat. 480): (*a*) La Musique (bars 51–6); (*b*) La Conversation (Bars 166–4); (*c*) Comus (bars 520–32; (*d*) Le Jeu (bars 670–81) (xi. 71, 72^{v}–73, 76, 78)

(Let everything yield to the sweetness of my charming harmonies)

(Uncommon heavenly child! Don't you understand me?
True enough, my tongue is a bit lively, but I'm just at
the point of speaking more quietly)

(If you'll only stop arguing, I'll give you both some chocolate!)

(If cards, dice the innocent trou-madame, billiards,
checkers, backgammon, chess, raffles, and jacks
cannot assuage your souls' sorrows, you will never
see the end of our trials!)

Les Arts florissants, composed for the musicians of Mlle de Guise, has a more interesting libretto and, overall, much better music than *Les Plaisirs de Versailles*. The drama involves the old argument among the arts as to which is the most valuable. Music, Poetry, Painting, and Architecture (ostensibly flourishing under the rule of peace, thanks to the beneficent exploits of Louis XIV) are the arts in question; they are listened to with interest by a Chorus of Warriors, just returned from battle. Suddenly Discord, jealous of the King's glory, and his Chorus of Furies appear; he threatens 'disputes, seditions, violence, vengeance, and rage'. From heaven the goddess Peace arrives; she tries to oust the interlopers, without success, but finally manages to call down on them Jupiter's thunderbolts, and they vanish. Peace urges the arts to join in pleasant harmony. They do, in a long paean to her divine intercession; at the close, she ascends, singing, to the heavens.

This scenario (or the unknown writer who built the libretto around it) provided Charpentier with splendid opportunities for the contrasts and diversity he so admired, while at the same time inviting the formal symmetries and *rondeau*-like refrain patterns that organize so elegantly (and integrate so powerfully) his best works. The opening solo of Music (a soprano) is a beguiling air–recitative–air (A b A) with two-viol ritornellos gracing the air (in G), basso continuo alone the recitative (in C). The Warriors (à 5) respond to it, saying how pleasant it is to hear such harmonious accents after the horrible sounds of war; the latter are embodied by Charpentier in a sword-rattling, musket-popping *stile concitato*. After Poetry (soprano), Painting (*haute-contre*—the part composed by Charpentier for himself), and Architecture (soprano) have successively had their say, the Warriors repeat their chorus, to round off Scene 1. A 'Bruit effroyable'—an angry flurry of rattling strings—introduces Discord (low tenor, more like a *basse chantante*); his solo is a tongue-twisting splatter of threats: it only *seems* to be a perpetual-motion line, for Charpentier—uncannily anticipating Mozart in Don Giovanni's 'Finch'han dal vino'—knows precisely when he must give the singer a moment's rest here and there. Peace (soprano) tries gently to dissuade Discord from carrying out his threats; he only redoubles them. Peace's call for help to Jupiter is rewarded by thunderbolts which rain down in torrents of viol runs, precipitating Discord and the Furies to Hell. In an ineffably sweet fourth scene with a symmetrical plan—(1) Prelude (minuet for the viols), (2) strophic air for Peace (another minuet), (3) a different 'Menuet des instruments'—Peace calls on the arts to return. They do, to conclude the opera with song and dancing to a long, imaginatively varied *chaconne en rondeau*, capped by yet another *rondeau*-like choral and instrumental finale.

Tragedies

Charpentier's operatic works culminated with three immense *tragédies en musique*, each in the form which Lully had established: a prologue and a five-act drama, complete with choruses, dances, an overture to introduce the prologue, orchestral preludes to the other acts, programmatic *symphonies*, and entr'acte orchestral *airs*. As mentioned earlier, Charpentier composed two of these—*Celse Martyr* (1687) and *David et Jonathas* (1688)—for the Jesuit Collège Louis-le Grand,[7] the other—*Médée* (1693)—for the Opéra.

Although the music of *Celse Martyr* has not survived, the libretto, by the Jesuit priest Père François de Paule Bretonneau, was published, as was that—also by him—for *David et Jonathas*. Its music is extant, but only in a score copied in 1690 by the King's music librarian, André-Danican Philidor, 'l'aîné'. The bitter tale of the death in battle of both Jonathan, David's dearest friend, and Saul, the Israelite king (and Jonathan's father), is spun out by the Jesuit librettist into a long, symbol-laden drama, and Charpentier did not find it easy to enliven musically the rather neutral characters shaped by Père Bretonneau. For once, however, an operatic prologue of the time is neither allegorical nor irrelevant to the drama: here, Saul tricks the witch of Endor into raising Samuel from the dead and, to his dismay, hears from Samuel's ghost the dreadful prophecy of his own death and that of Jonathan, as well as the inheritance of his kingdom by David. Charpentier's setting of the music for 'L'Ombre de Samüel' (a deep bass) is ghostly indeed: bass violins (and continuo) à 4—nothing else. Notable in the opera proper are the big *rondeau*-like structures Charpentier creates through varied reprises of material by different forces (as in both

[7] Charpentier's work for the Jesuit college is treated in Lowe, *Marc-Antoine Charpentier*.

scene i of Act I, with Warriors set off from Captives, and scene iii of Act II, for Saul and a Chorus of Philistines) and several stunning fugal preludes (to Saul's air 'Objet d'une implacable haine' in Act III, scene ii; to David's *récit* 'Souverain juge des mortels', which opens Act IV). By far the most telling music, however, is saved for Act V and the tragic climax of the work. Jonathan is mortally wounded, and this evokes from Saul an agonized reaction which is underscored by a choral murmur, 'Hélas! hélas!', repeated like a tolling bell. Jonathan dies in David's arms, their last exchange of fealty coloured mournfully by two recorders, to which soft strings are added for David's poignant lament, 'Jamais amour plus fidèle et plus tendre' (echoed by the chorus). Saul's death (by his own hand), too, is handled by Charpentier in an exceptionally sensitive recitative. The succeeding (and final) 'Marche triomphante' and chorus celebrating David's ascendancy ('Chantons sa gloire!') is, we suppose, unavoidable; it comes, nevertheless, as an intrusive anti-climax and challenges our suspension of disbelief in the musical drama as a whole.

Médée is a finer composition in every respect, a superb work of musical theatre and every bit the equal of Lully's best (and some consider it superior, in invention and careful detail).[8] The obligatory prologue, with 'bergers héroiques' and allegorical/mythological figures—La Victoire, La Gloire, and Bellone (the Roman goddess of war)—lauding the King and his 'peaceable reign', is no small work in itself, at more than seven hundred bars, including its French overture (scored à 5, in the Lullian manner). Thomas Corneille's treatment of the Greek myth results in an original and psychologically complex libretto. It centres on Jason's faithlessness to, and betrayal of, Medea (who had fled her own country with him after he acquired the Golden Fleece, and had borne his children) and her murders of their children, of Creon king of Corinth, and of Creüsa, Creon's daughter and Jason's mistress. Charpentier's aptitude for exploiting dramatic possibilities, and his skill at embodying musically shades of feeling and emotion, are especially striking. So too is his orchestral writing, more colourful and careful than ever. (Fortunately, the score printed by Ballard in 1694 is

---

[8] An especially rich source of information and opinion on *Médée* is the complete issue of *L'Avant-scène opéra*, 68 (Oct. 1984), dedicated to the opera, with a complete libretto and essays and analyses by more than a dozen authors.

unusually replete with the kinds of precise indications that characterize the composer's autographs, for no manuscript survives.)

We have hardly been introduced to Medea, at the opening of Act I, before Charpentier plunges us deep into her passionate and proud, jealous and fierce character. He undergirds her first *récit* ('S'il me vole son cœur, si la princesse y règne, | De plus grands efforts feront voir | Ce qu'est Médée et son pouvoir') with a unique throbbing string-orchestra accompaniment, and he frames her speech (which establishes the theme of the whole drama) with stormy, rushing passage-work—a kind of 'angry' music which will return a number of times later, seeming to forecast insistently the drama's foreordained conclusion (Ex. 32).

In later acts, other facets of Medea's personality are revealed: her attempts to act with compassion as a mother (in Act II) and with generosity as a wife (in Act III), and also her malignant sorcery (in the ariosos 'Noires filles du Styx' and 'Dieu du Cocyte et des royaumes sombres' of Act III, both accompanied darkly and balefully by low strings, menacingly muted). The music for her appearances in Acts IV and V presents her as increasingly seized with rage, ever nearer the edge of madness. Her final ferocious adieu to Jason finds her over the edge; it is

Ex. 32. *Médée* (Cat. 491), excerpt from Act I, scene i, bars 89–107
(Paris: C. Ballard, 1694), 5–7

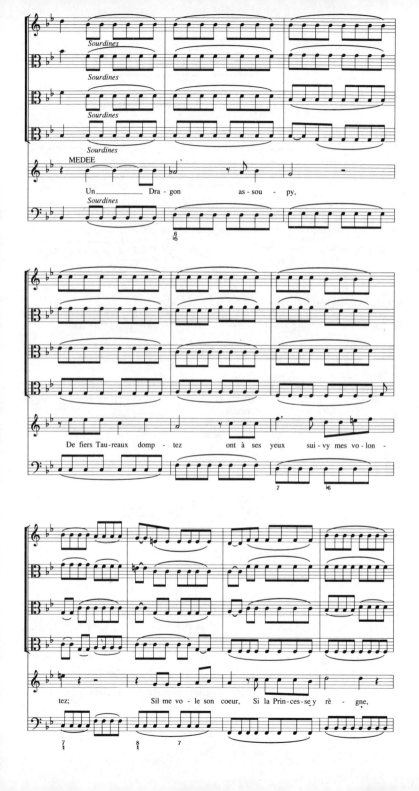

De plus grands ef - forts_____ fe - ront voir Ce qu'est Mé -

dée et son pou - voir.

(A docile dragon, Proud bulls tamed, have done my will
before his very eyes; If he steals his heart from me, If the
Princess reigns over it, The most dreadful deeds will show
What Medea is, and her power.)

introduced and followed by the 'angry' string music that has
become identified with her, and is the last sound we hear in the
opera.

Charpentier applies similar dramatic sensitivity and precise
characterization to others in the drama, often through unusual
vocal combinations or instrumental scoring. In the song-and-

dance divertissement that concludes Act I, for example, he distinguishes between the Chorus of Corinthians (initially offstage: a nice *coup de théâtre* and a great novelty—anticipated, it should be said, in *David et Jonathas*), which he composes à 4, from the Chorus of Argives, à 3. The divertissement that closes Act II is a fantasy in which the nubile Creüsa is addressed by Cupid and 'Captifs d'Amour de diverses nations' (including Italy, of course, as an excuse for an aria, 'Chi teme d'amore', more Italianate than the Italians'); it ends with a *passacaille en rondeau* for orchestra and chorus, the full chorus à 5 alternating with a *petit chœur* à 3 that is enchantingly reminiscent, in its airiness and dancing lightness, of sixteenth-century chanson style. Act IV begins with a delicately chromatic prelude for two recorders, two violins, and continuo—our introduction to Creüsa clad in the deceptively beautiful poisoned robe given her by Medea. In the same act, there is a striking love scene for Creüsa and Jason: lyrical solos for each (*airs sérieux*, really) open the scene; they become more and more impassioned, and the dialogue ends with a brief, wistful duet. Creon concludes the act with a despairing *récit* ('Noires divinités, que voulez-vous de moi?'); Charpentier takes his cue from lines that refer to the abyss into which Medea threatens to hurl Creon, and aims for the deepest and darkest possible orchestral sonority: omitting the *dessus de violon* entirely and dividing the basses in two parts, he creates a literally abysmal accompaniment of low strings. Act V has the most violent contrasts of all—between rage (Medea) and lamentation (the Corinthian Chorus, mourning Creon), hopeless love (Jason and Creüsa) and poignant death (Creüsa's). Perhaps what remains longest in the memory is the magnificent lament of the Corinthians, which begins 'Ah! funeste revers! fortune impitoyable! | Corinthe hélas! que vas-tu devenir?' (Ex. 33). With its Italianate curve of melody and richness of harmony, but also its careful declamation and subtle word repetitions ('fortune', 'hélas'), not to mention its undeniable evocation of Lully's celebrated choral lament, 'Alceste est morte!', this chorus exemplifies perfectly Charpentier's reconciliation and synthesis of the Italian and French sources of his art.

(Ah! fatal misfortune, pitiless fate!
Corinth, alas! what will become of you?)

SELECT BIBLIOGRAPHY

ANTHONY, JAMES R., *French Baroque Music from Beaujoyeulx to Rameau* (rev. edn., New York: W. W. Norton; London: B. T. Batsford, Ltd., 1978).

BROSSARD, SÉBASTIEN DE, 'Catalogue des livres de musique théorique et pratique, vocale et instrumentale, tant imprimée que manuscrite, qui sont dans le cabinet du Sr Sebastien de Brossard Chanoine de Meaux, dont il supplie très humblement sa Majesté d'accepter le don, pour être mis et conservés dans sa Bibliothèque. Fait et écrit en l'année 1724', *F-Pn* MS Rés. Vm^8 21.

BURKE, J. R., 'Marc-Antoine Charpentier (*c*. 1634–1704): Sources of Style in the Liturgical Works', Ph.D. thesis (Oxford, 1985).

CESSAC, CATHERINE, *Marc-Antoine Charpentier* (Paris: Librairie Arthème Fayard, 1988).

CHARPENTIER, MARC-ANTOINE. 'Mélanges autographes', *F-Pn* MS Rés. Vm^1 259 (28 vols.).

—— *Vocal Chamber Music*, ed. John S. Powell (Recent Researches in the Music of the Baroque Era, 48; Madison, Wisconsin: A-R Editions, Inc., 1986).

CRUSSARD, CLAUDE, *Un musicien français oublié: Marc-Antoine Charpentier* (Paris: Librairie Floury, 1945).

HITCHCOCK, H. WILEY, 'The Latin Oratorios of Marc-Antoine Charpentier', *Musical Quarterly*, 41 (1955), 41–65.

—— 'The Instrumental Music of Marc-Antoine Charpentier', *Musical Quarterly*, 47 (1961), 58–72.

—— 'Marc-Antoine Charpentier and the Comédie-Française', *Journal of the American Musicological Society*, 24 (1971), 255–81.

—— *Les Œuvres de/The Works of Marc-Antoine Charpentier: Catalogue raisonné* (Paris: A. et J. Picard, 1982).

—— 'Marc-Antoine Charpentier: Mémoire and Index', *Recherches sur la musique classique française*, 23 (1985), 5–44.

KÄSER, THEODOR, *Die Leçon de Ténèbres im 17. und 18. Jahrhundert* (Bern: Verlag Paul Hapt, 1966).

LE CERF DE LA VIÉVILLE, JEAN LAURENT, *Comparaison de la musique italienne et de la musique française* (Brussels, 1704–6; repr. Geneva: Editions Minkoff, 1972). 2nd edn. in Pierre Bourdelot and Jacques Bonnet, *Histoire de la musique et de ses effets* (Amsterdam, 1725; repr. Graz: Akademische Druck- und Verlagsamstalt, 1966).

LOWE, ROBERT W. *Marc-Antoine Charpentier et l'opéra de collége* (Paris: G. P. Maisonneuve & Larose, 1966).

'Marc Antoine Charpentier: *Médée*', *L'Avant-scène opéra*, 68 (Oct. 1984).

PARMLEY, ANDREW, 'The Secular Stage Works of Marc-Antoine Charpentier', Ph.D. Thesis (London, 1985).

POWELL, JOHN S. 'Charpentier's Music for Molière's *Le Malade imaginaire* and its Revisions', *Journal of the American Musicological Society*, 39 (1986), 87–142.

RANUM, PATRICIA. 'A Sweet Servitude: A Musician's Life at the Court of Mlle de Guise', *Early Music*, 15 (1987), 347–60.

RUFF, LILLIAN M. 'Marc-Antoine Charpentier's *Règles de composition*', *The Consort*, 24 (1967), 233–70.

TITON DU TILLET, *Description du Parnasse françois* (Paris: Jean Baptiste Coignard, 1727).

TUNLEY, DAVID, *The Eighteenth-Century French Cantata* (London: Dennis Dobson, 1974).

INDEX OF WORKS CITED

Numbers in parentheses are those assigned to the works of Charpentier in H. W. Hitchcock, *Les Œuvres de/The Works of Marc-Antoine Charpentier: Catalogue raisonné* (Paris, 1982).